but you don't look autistic at all

but you don't look autistic at all

bianca toeps

This book is an adaptation of the original Dutch version *Maar je ziet er helemaal niet autistisch uit*, published by Blossom Books, 2019

Cover design and photography: Bianca Toeps
Cover hair and makeup: Charlotte van Beusekom
Graphic design text: Studio L.E.O.
Translation: Fay MacCorquodale-Smith, Translate This
Proofreading: Natasha Ziada
Final checks: Maria van Loosdrecht, Iris van Hal and Jorrit Bosma

butyoudontlookautisticatall.com
@biancatoeps
#ButYouDontLookAutisticAtAll
#BYDLAAA

For interviews, speaking events or comments, reach out via
info@butyoudontlookautisticatall.com

If I had a chance to go back in time
I'd tell the younger me to breathe
Cause you'll be fine
Trust the path you're on and dream
Write down the words on your mind

Maria Mena, 'Interesting'

I would like to thank dad for his incredible bravery to work with me on this book. I would also like to thank Monique for letting me call her 'stepmother' in the interest of readability, even though she hates that word. I thank Riemer for his endless patience with me every time I was just done with writing. Thanks to Aafke for her encouragement and corrections, and for being my Big Example because she has written a book before. I would like to thank Blossom Books for their trust, because there's nothing better than a publisher who gets you and sometimes just writes "hahaha!" in the corrections. Thanks to Charlotte for the beautiful makeup on my cover and author photos. Thanks to all the people who I interviewed for this book, or who gave me snippets through Twitter.

A very special thanks for the English edition goes out to these generous supporters: Sven Hilbrants, Aisha Sie, Paul Rispens, The Young Family, Sander Begeer, Mark Sleper, Renske & Andreas, Gwen Landes, Dimitar Nedev, Josephiene Westdorp, Quinte Marijnissen, Annette, Owen Stock, Karin Glaudemans, Fumiko Miura, Javier Miranda Perez and Mariko Horioka.

ありがとうございます!

Table of contents

Intro: Invisibly different

You walk out of the aeroplane via the jet bridge. For the past ten hours, you've been sitting in a cramped seat, eating an undefinable meal and watching *Kung Fu Panda* because you didn't have anything better to do anyway. You wanted to sleep, but thanks to the baby three seats down that was only a partial success. Now you're here, on the other side of the world. Billboards are calling out incomprehensible messages and even the bathroom is something to behold with its thousands of buttons, bells and whistles. The musical note produces a noise that vaguely resembles cascading water and what you thought was the flush button turned out to be the setting to wash your bottom. A lukewarm trickle sprays upwards. Eeew.

Past customs you're being picked up. You hold out your hand, but the person in front of you doesn't take it. Instead, he bows. You try to make eye contact, but the man in uniform merely looks down. Just as you're about to open the taxi door, it opens by itself. From the back seat you look out the window covered in stickers, past the blaring television screen at the back of the headrest of the seat in front of you.

There are neon billboards everywhere. "Nihon e yokoso!", the driver says. Silence. The driver thinks for a second and then says, "Werukomu tsu Djapan!"

Within thirty minutes, you've probably broken dozens of social rules. You feel like an alien, like a bull in a proverbial china shop. You're tired and overstimulated because of all the signals that are fired at you. Signals you don't understand most of the time. Your saving grace: you're a for-eigner. You're clearly not Japanese, so nobody blames you for your mistakes.

But what if you do look Japanese? Ah, different story.

That's what autism feels like to me.

Autism, that's what I have.[1] You can't tell from the outside. So when I tell people about it, that's what I hear all the time: "But... you don't look autistic at all!"

---

1 More about te use of 'autistic' versus 'with autism' in chapter 7, part 7, on page 211.

Chapter 1

An alien in Tokyo

There I am, in Tokyo. The reason *you* feel like an alien here, is probably the exact reason why I feel so at ease. I'm an alien everywhere, but in Tokyo I have an excuse. A visible excuse for why I'm different – my 1.83 meter tall Western appearance. No one notices that my awkwardness usually isn't caused by my gaijin-ness (*gaijin* is the Japanese word for stranger, foreigner). It also helps that my autistic quirks – such as not looking people in the eye, my aversion to touch, and my love for trains that run on time (and have Quiet Zones that are actually quiet!) – are the most normal thing in the world here. The three months a year that I spend among the neon billboards in Japan are a period of well-deserved rest for me.

Now, it's not my intention to write a rhapsody on how amazing Japan is. I could go on about it for hours (because hey, autistic), but as far as I'm concerned you could just pick up a good old travel guide or look up the *Abroad in Japan, Only in Japan* and *Begin Japanology* videos on YouTube. This book is about autism.

Circus horse

"Autism – that's being able to count matches really fast and knowing that 7 August 1984 was a Tuesday, right?"

Most people have somewhat of an idea of what the term autism entails. If you yourself have autism, or know someone who is autistic, you probably have a pretty good understanding of it. If you got your information from TV, I'm not so sure.

In this age of advertising revenue, social media, and people with an average attention span of three seconds, network executives go for the extremes. When they're looking for a person with anorexia, they prefer someone who weighs twenty-eight kilos. Need a teen mom for TV? Only if she's living on home-brand energy drinks and roll-your-own cigarettes. And if the topic is autism, they want people who have recreated three German cities using model trains or built Eiffel towers out of toothpicks, someone who can draw an accurate picture of New York after a single helicopter flight, or at least someone who can, for any given date, calculate at lightning speed if it was a Tuesday or a Wednesday. Autistics on TV are often portrayed as some kind of circus horse.

If this is also your image of autism, I'm afraid I have to disappoint you. The only reason I know 7 August 1984 was a Tuesday is because it's the day I was born. I don't have any circus horse talents, and that goes for the majority of autistics. Also, I don't want to call every hobby that got out of hand a talent, because anyone can become good at building

Eiffel towers if they have the luxury of spending a thousand hours doing that due to a lack of work or social life.

While one autistic person builds Eiffel towers, the other one struggles to fit in at work. Just as complicated most of the time, but a lot less visible. Maybe that is my talent: to appear normal. I've gotten pretty good at it by now, if I say so myself.

Autism according to the DSM-5

The criteria for an autism diagnosis are described in the DSM-5, the 5th edition of The Diagnostic and Statistical Manual of Mental Disorders (or the Junior Woodchucks' Guidebook, but for psychiatrists).[2]

DSM-5 Autism Spectrum Disorder - Diagnostic Criteria

A Persistent deficits in social communication and social interaction across multiple contexts, as manifested by the following, currently or by history (examples are illustrative, not exhaustive; see text):

1. **Deficits in social-emotional reciprocity**, ranging, for example, from abnormal social approach and failure of normal back-and-forth conversation; to reduced sharing of interests, emotions, or affect; to failure to initiate or respond to social interactions.
2. **Deficits in nonverbal communicative behaviors used for social interaction**, ranging, for

---

2 In this book, we cite from the Diagnostic and Statistical Manual of Mental Disorders, fifth edition, by the American Psychiatric Association. That's why some words, for example "behavior", are spelled differently.

example, from poorly integrated verbal and nonverbal communication; to abnormalities in eye contact and body language or deficits in understanding and use of gestures; to a total lack of facial expressions and nonverbal communication.

3. **Deficits in developing, maintaining, and understanding relationships**, ranging, for example, from difficulties adjusting behavior to suit various social contexts; to difficulties in sharing imaginative play or in making friends; to absence of interest in peers.

B Restricted, repetitive patterns of behavior, interests, or activities, as manifested by at least two of the following, currently or by history (examples are illustrative, not exhaustive; see text):

1. **Stereotyped or repetitive motor movements, use of objects, or speech** (e.g., simple motor stereotypes, lining up toys or flipping objects, echolalia, idiosyncratic phrases).
2. **Insistence on sameness, inflexible adherence to routines, or ritualized patterns of verbal or nonverbal behavio**r (e.g., extreme distress at small changes, difficulties with transitions, rigid thinking patterns, greeting

rituals, need to take same route or eat same food every day).

3. **Highly restricted, fixated interests that are abnormal in intensity or focus** (e.g., strong attachment to or preoccupation with unusual objects, excessively circumscribed or perseverative interests).

4. **Hyper- or hyporeactivity to sensory input or unusual interest in sensory aspects of the environment** (e.g., apparent indifference to pain/temperature, adverse response to specific sounds or textures, excessive smelling or touching of objects, visual fascination with lights or movement).

C Symptoms must be present in the early developmental period (but may not become fully manifest until social demands exceed limited capacities, or may be masked by learned strategies in later life).

D Symptoms cause clinically significant impairment in social, occupational, or other important areas of current functioning.

E These disturbances are not better explained by intellectual disability (intellectual developmental disorder) or global developmental delay.

In short, what it comes down to is that someone who has autism has trouble with communication and social interaction and has typical behaviours and interests. This must have been the case your entire life, it has to be a real burden and there can't be any other underlying cause.

I'll go into the aforementioned symptoms in more detail later, but there's one issue I'd like to point out here: this list is clearly based on a neurotypical (non-autistic) person's point of view. The limitations in communication and social interaction are listed at the top as the most important characteristics, because those are what an outsider notices first. Of course, that outsider, being the psychiatrist, is also the one making the diagnosis. But if you ask autistic people what they struggle with most, it's usually overstimulation (the last point in category B) they mention first.

ASDF#%$#TF?

If you're thinking, I've heard of autism, but also of Asperger, ASD, PDD-NOS – what does it all mean? Since the DSM-5 came out, everything has been called 'autism spectrum disorder' (ASD). As a consequence, Asperger and PDD-NOS no longer exist as diagnoses but have been included in the umbrella term 'autism'.

Multidimensional vector space

Autism is referred to as a spectrum disorder, which indicates that the disorder has a range, from lower-functioning to higher-functioning autistics. This view might be a bit too straight-forward, however. Because would someone who doesn't speak but does build complex compu-ter models be considered a higher-functioning or lower-functioning autistic? Autistics' capa-cities are usually disharmonic, which – simply put – means they're unevenly distributed. A person who seems to manage in everyday life may be experiencing mental problems that make life nearly unbearable. So autism isn't necessarily a line from zero to a hundred, but rather a multidimensional vector space. Go and look that up in a maths textbook.

The Theory of Mind (and why it's shit)

There's a little girl sitting opposite a stern-looking lady wearing a plaid blazer. Her parents told her she was going to play, but instead of colouring, she has to listen to this woman. The woman has two plastic dolls in her hands. "This is Sally", she says, while showing the girl one of the dolls. "And this is Anne."

Sally has a marble in her basket. Anne has a box. The girl wonders why.

"One day Sally and Anne are playing with the marble in their house", the woman in the plaid blazer says. The girl is confused. She doesn't see a house and it isn't clear to her on which day Sally and Anne are playing. So far there's been no playing at all. She still wants to colour.

"Sally is going outside now", says the woman. The girl looks at her lips. She's wearing lipstick. Orange. The woman puts the Sally doll under the table. The girl doesn't understand: wasn't she going outside?

"Anne is naughty and moves the marble to her box", the orange lips say. The little girl is startled: being naughty is wrong! Meanwhile orange-lip-woman lifts Sally up onto the table, then asks the girl, "Where will Sally look for her marble?"

The girl thinks. What's going on here? Why is Sally looking for her marble? Did she lose it? Cautiously, the girl looks toward the basket. Orange lipstick doesn't respond. The marble is in the box, the girl knows that.

"Where will Sally look for her marble?" the lips ask once

more. If she wants to *find* the marble she should look in Anne's box, the girl thinks. She carefully points at the box. The analyst seems content with that answer, because she continues on to the next question. The girl still wants to colour. Something with orange. A tangerine, or the sun, at night. The girl has autism, and according to this examination she lacks Theory of Mind.

Scientists have been searching for an explanation for autism for ages. Some with the desire to "cure" us autistics or, even creepier, eradicate us, as if we're back to the eugenics of the 1930s. Others are mainly trying to understand us, with varying degrees of success. In the first half of the twentieth century for instance, people believed mothers of autistic children didn't give their offspring enough love. Thankfully that theory has been banished to the realm of fairy tales, although, as you will find out further on in this book, we never seem to get rid of it completely.

Nowadays, the leading theory is that autistics have difficulty with the Theory of Mind, the ability to realise that other people think or feel differently than we do. The Theory of Mind model was first presented in 1985 by researchers Alan Leslie, Uta Frith and Simon Baron-Cohen. (If you're thinking, huh? Borat? No, that's Sacha Baron-Cohen, his cousin.)

In the research that led to the Theory of Mind model, the Sally-Anne play was performed for a few children. Autistic children answered the question where Sally would look for her marble wrong more often than the control group.

Baron-Cohen and his colleagues concluded that autistics can't put themselves in someone else's place.

More precisely: according to them, people with autism don't realise that other people think differently than they do and are unable to observe their own thoughts. It would explain why most autistics don't play games such as 'playing house', and why it's believed they can't lie. Personally, I have always had my doubts about this theory, as do many other autistics.

I still remember how upset I was when my mother explained to me what Sinéad O'Connor's 'Nothing Compares 2 U' is about. The song, which is about the sadness of an abandoned lover, was a hit in February of 1990; I was five years old back then. I also remember my mother asking me why I was crying, and making up a story about bumping into the table. It was probably the least credible lie ever, but it was still a reflection of my Theory of Mind. After all, I *was* trying to trick my mother.

To this day I can get overwhelmed by other people's emotions at the silliest, most unexpected moments – during a visit to 'Plopsaland' (a children's theme park in Belgium), for example. My ex-boyfriend Mark and I went there for my twenty-sixth birthday because K3 was going to perform there. Together we had been watching the TV show in which the kiddie pop band went looking for a replacement for band member Kathleen, and we wanted to see how Josje, the winner, would do at a live performance. While devouring a pizza, long before the gig was supposed to start, the music suddenly started. K3 appeared on stage. All kids jumped up, eyes the size of dinner plates. "Relax, sit down, it's just a quick soundcheck!", Karen shouted into her mic. And me? I was crying.

Before you think I'm an obsessed K3 fan and that *that* was the reason I burst into tears: it wasn't. It was the chil-drens' emotions as they were suddenly surprised by their idols. It was the music. It was the whole picture that was so overwhelming it suddenly made me emotional. Mark already knew me quite well by then, but I found it quite embarrassing myself. I hunched over my pizza, pulled my cap a little further down and pretended everything was fine.

And that's often what I do. Close myself off. Turn away. I refused to come along to the Dutch classic 'Soldier of Orange', not because I hate musicals, but because I didn't want to be confronted with the emotions. I dread auntie Mary's birthday because I know I'll be overwhelmed by the three big kisses, the loud laughter and the smell of buckets of old-lady perfume.

All autistics I know recognise this. We close ourselves off to stimuli, and then get blamed for not having any empathy. For not understanding auntie Mary's good intentions. But to what extent does auntie Mary understand us? To what extent does she accept that our way of processing stimuli is different from hers?

A double empathy problem

In 2007 a silverback gorilla named Bokito escaped from Blijdorp Zoo in Rotterdam. He attacked a woman, who sustained hundreds of bites, various broken bones and a shattered hand. The woman was under the impression she had a special bond with the ape: he "smiled" at her and made eye contact. That by making eye contact she was provoking Bokito never occurred to her. Not even after the zoo staff's repeated warnings.

The misinterpretation of animal behaviour is a well-known phenomenon. Pet owners, for example, often project their own feelings and thoughts onto their pets, and you can hear them say things like "my cat is really stubborn" or "my dog felt guilty". According to Damian Milton, a researcher at the University of Kent, a similar difference occurs between autistics and neurotypicals: the double empathy problem.[3]

People like to fill in thoughts and emotions for others. They do this based on their own experiences: "After hearing news like that I'd cry, so if you don't, that means you feel less sadness." Even though Milton's theory poses that the empathy problem works both ways (hence the word double), it's the neurotypicals of this world who determine the desired, "normal" reaction to all sorts of events and emotions. It's the neurotypicals who are in the majority and therefore determine

3 Milton, Damian E.M. ,'On the ontological status of autism: the 'double empathy problem', *Disability & Society*, 27:6, 883-887, 2012. DOI: 10.1080/09687599.2012.710008

how we view autism. As an autistic, I often feel forced to *code-switch*, to switch between two different types of behaviour: my own and that which is socially desirable.

When I went to Japan for the first time, I noticed that a lot of what I considered to be set rules and concepts was different there. Looking people in the eye, polite? Absolutely not. A bit of noise creates a nice atmosphere? Nope, it's antisocial. Slurping noodles, gross? Not at all, it makes the noodles taste extra good! I realised what Milton also concluded in his research paper: social reality is a construct, a set of rules that the players determine together.

This is also at the core of the problem with the Theory of Mind experiment by Baron-Cohen and associates, which recently received some criticism. The experiment takes place in a social setting created by and according to the standards of neurotypical people. That will inherently affect the results. Analysis of video recordings shows that the researchers don't pick up on certain non-verbal signals displayed by the autistic children[4]. This causes the children to doubt themselves and adjust their answers. Children with autism are often taught not to trust their own feelings, so I'm not surprised they say what the researcher appears to want to hear. The interpretation of the results is littered with neurotypical

---

4 Korkiakangas, T., Dindar, K., Laitila, A. en Kärnä, E., 'The Sally–Anne test: an interactional analysis of a dyadic assessment.' *International Journal of Language & Communication Disorders*, 51: 685-702, 2016. DOI:10.1111/1460-6984.12240

assumptions as well. But a researcher who thinks that someone who doesn't answer questions according to neurotypical standards has a problem, is the one with a lack of understanding, in my opinion.

Autistics among each other usually have far fewer communication problems. We find each other online, recognise each other's struggles and talents and form friendships in which we don't have to wear masks, where it's okay not to go to someone's birthday and where no one is shocked by blunt remarks. And even in these friendships I sometimes feel insecure. Insecure because the neurotypical behaviour has been so exhaustingly pounded into me, I sometimes honestly don't know who I am anymore.

The Intense World Theory (and why it is *the* shit)

The Theory of Mind model mainly focuses on differences in communication from the neurotypical point of view. Milton's double empathy problem gives an explanation for the difference in communication, but we still have quite some way to go. We have a different neurotype, a different way of processing information, but why? And how do you explain someone's love for trains, hypersensitivity to certain textures or aversion to bright lights and loud noises?

A more inclusive, more comprehensive explanation can be found in the Intense World Theory, a theory that has been gaining more credence in the past few years. The founders of this theory, neuroscientists Henry and Kamila Markram, have an autistic son. Their findings resonate with what a lot of autistic people actually already know: the autistic brain is hyperactive.

According to the Markrams, more connections are being made in the autistic brain and brain cells respond more emphatically to each other. There's a stronger response to stimuli, thoughts run rampant quicker. In short: the world is extremely intense for autistics.

That doesn't just explain autistic people's hypersensitivity, but also their apparent *in*sensitivity and limitations in social communication. We close up in the overwhelming storm of stimuli, like a computer that freezes when you give it ten different tasks at the same time. Then our hyper-fanatic brains make sure we remember that scary, nasty experience very well and will try to avoid it in the future.

Or, as the Markrams explain in their scientific publication from 2010:

> *"The intense world that the autistic person faces could also easily become aversive if the amygdala and related emotional areas are significantly affected with local hyper-functionality. The lack of social interaction in autism may therefore not be because of deficits in the ability to process social and emotional cues, but because a sub-set of cues are overly intense, compulsively attended to, excessively processed and remembered with frightening clarity and intensity. Typical autistic symptoms, such as averted eye gaze, social withdrawal, and lack of communication, may be explained by an initial over-awareness of sensory and social fragments of the environment, which may be so intense, that avoidance is the only refuge."*[5]

An abundance of stimuli can be tricky, but there's an upside to it. Autistics tend to have a very good eye for detail and a knack for logic. Where neurotypical brains usually choose

---

5 Markram, K. and Markram, H., 'The Intense World Theory – A Unifying Theory of the Neurobiology of Autism', *Frontiers in Human Neuroscience*, 4, 2010. DOI: 10.3389/fnhum.2010.00224.

the well-trodden paths (which are quicker, but as such more prone to generalizations and preconceptions), autistic brains explore every little side street and country road. For this reason a relatively large number of autistics work in science and IT, among colleagues who may not be autistic, but do possess a lot of the same traits. The Markrams argue that more autistics could use their potential if their environment would enable them to do so.

Instead of showering autistics with stimuli so they 'learn how to deal with it' or drilling them like soldiers, they argue for a calm, predictable environment for autistic children, so they are less likely to close up or develop anxieties. This way they can develop the positive aspects of their amped-up brain.

In their own words:

> *"Behavioural treatment according to the Intense World Theory is proposed to focus on filtering the extremes in the intensity of all sensory and emotional exposure as well as relaxation and progressive systematic desensitization to stimuli presentation. The probably most counter-intuitive suggestion that emerges from the Intense World Theory is to surround the child with a highly predictable and calm environment protected from abrupt sensory and emotional transients and surprises for the first years of life to*

prevent excessive sensory and emotion driven brain development."[6]

So, as it turns out, the old Dutch saying of 'calmness, cleanliness and consistency' is not so silly after all.

Uta Frith, one of the scientists on team Theory of Mind, felt this new theory breathing down her neck and decided to make herself look like a complete fool once and for all. On spectrumnews.org, the website that calls itself 'the leading source of news and expert opinion' in the field of autism, she wrote:

"Our particular concern regarding the Intense World Theory centers on drastic suggested treatments for individuals with autism, namely withdrawing stimulation during infancy. The Markrams do not merely hint at such interventions, but explicitly spell them out. Yet if the theory is incorrect, these treatments could be damaging. As studies of Romanian orphans have strikingly shown, insufficient stimulation and impoverished neuronal input in early development are damaging to children's social, cognitive and emotional functioning."[7]

6 Markram, K. en Markram, H., 'The Intense World Theory – A Unifying Theory of the Neurobiology of Autism', *Frontiers in Human Neuroscience*, 4, 2010. DOI: 10.3389/fnhum.2010.00224.
7 Frith, Uta and Remington, Anna, 'Intense World Theory Raises Intense Worries', 2014. https://www.spectrumnews.org/opinion/viewpoint/intense-world-theory-raises-intense-worries/

Sure, Uta. A low-stimulus environment can TOTALLY be compared to a Romanian orphanage. A tip for Uta: that was sarcasm. Just thought I'd clarify that, because for someone who calls herself an expert on the Theory of Mind she has a very poor understanding of what the Markrams mean.

Chapter 2

The DSM and I

Back to the DSM-5. Let's size me up, just like several care organisations have done, multiple times.

Social stuff

A Persistent deficits in social communication and social interaction across multiple contexts.

Is everything alright?!

 1 Deficits in social-emotional reciprocity, ranging, for example, from abnormal social approach and failure of normal back-and-forth conversation; to reduced sharing of interests, emotions, or affect; to failure to initiate or respond to social interactions.

I regularly face communication problems, although the intensity varies from day to day. On good days I skip merrily down the street, say good morning to the bus driver, point out to someone they've dropped their ticket and smoothly order the most complicated drink off the Starbucks menu. On days like that, it seems like I don't even have autism. I'm spontaneous, cheerful and fun.

However, there are also days where I can't even muster a simple 'hello'. For example, the other day an old lady in my yoga class gave me a dirty look because I didn't say good morning back to her. I had wanted to, but my brain felt like my mother's old iMac that's still trying to run High Sierra. By the time I realised the woman had said something and I had to respond (but how?), several seconds had passed and I already felt her angry stare. "Oh, ehm, good morning...", I mumbled. "Rude youngster!" I heard the woman think.

In Japan I don't notice what kind of autistic mood I'm in until I have to place my order at the Starbucks counter. It's the first moment in the day where I need to talk. On a good day my order rolls of the tongue in fluent Japanese, on a mediocre day I merely vocalise some sounds, at which point the staff quickly switches to English (which then really bums me out) and on a bad day I start to sweat, my voice cracks and I wonder why they don't have robots or at least installed touch screens. And that's just ordering a chai tea latte. Communication is so much more. Body language. Unspoken rules. Subtle hints. As a child I wasn't able to deal with these dimensions at all, but I've learnt to through trial and error. There's a constant alarm going off inside my head, though.

"IS EVERYTHING ALRIGHT?!" my brain shouts every ten seconds as I walk through the mall with my Japanese friend Kei. I'm trying to monitor if she's still having a good time with me, if I'm talking too much, or not enough. The alarm bells are working overtime and apparently it shows, because then it's actually Kei who asks me if everything is alright. "Yeah, yeah, fine!" I respond without thinking. "If you're not okay just wait outside. I'll quickly get what I need and I'll meet you there right after!" I tell her that's not necessary while feeling quite annoyed with myself. Although I told her about my autism, the fact that she can tell feels like failing.

I was also having a hard time during my work on the editorial crew of a TV show. Every break I was sitting there staring at my sandwich; it was as if I kept ending up in the wrong place, in between two conversations. My alarm bells were going off non-stop: "Say something! Ask something!" But what are you supposed to ask? Often when I tried to contribute to the conversation, I couldn't get a word in edgewise. When there finally was a pause in the conversation, the subject had already changed three times.

Week after week I wondered if it was me. It must be, I thought. I'm the one with autism. It wasn't until much later that I realised the rest of the team possibly shared some of the blame. Maybe they were just as unable to involve me as I was to get myself involved.

TIP:
COMMUNICATING WITH AUTISTICS

How do you talk to an autistic? First of all, one question at a time, please. When over-stimulated, my boyfriend Riemer struggles to recognise questions that don't actually end in a question mark. I'm sometimes left waiting for an answer for several minutes after a sentence that ended in "...if that's okay with you." That's not a question, according to Riemer.

If you want to have a chat with me, you could ask me for some tips. On the best places to go shopping in Tokyo, for example. Or which documentaries I'd recommend. If you notice I'm having a hard time getting the words out, you could also decide to tell something *yourself*.

If someone else takes the lead, my hyper-alert brain can get some rest. I love enthusiastic people – if I know why something makes you happy, I get that, even if I personally couldn't care less about Toto, B&M roller coasters or gold records. Most autistics I know hate small talk and would rather dive straight in. We'd rather listen to you go on and on about your collection of Star Wars cards than to chit-chat about the weather.

Is there something important you'd like to discuss with me? Email me or send me a text.

This gives me time to think things over, which helps me protect my boundaries and get my points across clearly. Older people tend to say you shouldn't argue via text message because it doesn't convey any emotions. But in fact, that's exactly the advantage of text. Plus, if you *do* want to convey emotions, they've come up with something very clever for that: emoji. This, too, is typical for most autistics I know. We joke about it amongst each other: "A phone you can make calls with? Who'd want *that*?"

Look at me when I'm talking to you!

2 Deficits in nonverbal communicative behaviors used for social interaction, ranging, for example, from poorly integrated verbal and nonverbal communication; to abnormalities in eye contact and body language or deficits in understanding and use of gestures; to a total lack of facial expressions and nonverbal communication.

We're going to jump back in time a little. I was twelve. I had missed swimming practice for the umpteenth time. My clubmates were bullies and I was the slowest one in the whole club. This was hardly surprising: every day, I threw my two mandatory ham sandwiches in the bin because I didn't like them. The saltiness prickled my tongue in such a nasty way I'd rather not eat at all. Once I got home I didn't have the energy to drag myself to the swimming pool. So every training day, I counted on my parents to forget the time. I 'forgot' the time as well, until it was definitely too late to go. Then I'd creep downstairs, ready for my lecture.

"Look at me when I'm talking to you!" my stepmother would say sternly. It felt as if her eyes were cutting through me like laser beams, like in a superhero movie or a cartoon. I'd fight my reflexes, reflexes that'd keep moving my head to the side and my eyes toward the ground. I'd force my chin up and squint my eyes until they were no more than slits. I no longer heard the words that came out of her mouth. They moved past me like smoke circles that slowly but surely transformed into wisps whose original shape you could no longer discern. Until I was startled by the next reprimand: "Don't give me that arrogant look!" I didn't even know what arrogant meant. I just wanted to show that I was listening.

Section A2 in the DSM is, among other things, about abnormal behaviour regarding eye contact. Brain scans show that in autistics, heightened activity can be measured in their emotional circuits when they're shown pictures of eyes or faces.[8] So making eye contact actually *is* more intense for them.

8 Dalton K.M., Nacewicz B.M., Johnstone T., et al. 'Gaze fixation and the neural circuitry of face processing in autism', *Nature neuroscience*, 8 (4): 519-526, 2005. DOI:10.1038/nn1421.

Looking people in the eye still isn't a hobby of mine. I once saw a video of myself – a TV interview about my work as a hand model – in which my eyes moved from side to side as if they were following a tennis match. I promised myself I'd mind that better in the future. I looked so... autistic.

Because I'm also pretty bad at remembering faces (perhaps because, in order to remember a face, you do need to look at it), I now try to combine looking at someone with remembering specific features that person has. "Ah, blue eyes, thick eyebrows, a little like Cara Delevingne." It still happens a little too often that I have ab-so-lute-ly no idea what the person I spoke to looked like. My flatmate in Tokyo for example – he's Portuguese and studies robotics, that much I know. But what he looks like? Uh, tall, I think. Yes, he must be, because the shoes in the wardrobe are quite large. Brown hair? Well done Toeps, you have just described pretty much every tall Portuguese guy. I wouldn't recognise him if I ran into him in the supermarket.

The last few years I have a little scene ready that I act out. "Sorry, super busy, I have a lot on my mind, you know what it's like!" I play the chaotic business woman, a more widely accepted persona than the evasive autistic. As soon as the person in front of me has told me their name, I quickly blurt out some facts about them. This way I try to prove that I really do know who I have in front of me. Luckily I have a good memory.

TIP:
DON'T TAKE IT PERSONALLY

To all neurotypicals who like to be looked in the eye: when an autistic doesn't look you in the eye, it's not a sign that they're not trustworthy or that they're being disrespectful. In the autistic community there's a meme that's shared a lot: "Do you want me to listen, or do you want me to pretend I'm listening?" Your message usually comes across better if the autistic in question doesn't look you in the eye.

If you're a parent or a teacher and you want to discipline a child, try to keep listening while you're lecturing. Why did the autistic child do that thing you're angry about? Maybe he or she had a good reason. Nothing hurt me more as a child than being punished while I thought I was doing the right thing.

Don't be too easily insulted. If an autistic doesn't recognise you in the street, that doesn't mean you haven't made an impression. He or she probably just has difficulty connecting one context to another. You don't expect someone who belongs in the library at a carnival. Duh.

I'm not here to make friends

3 Deficits in developing, maintaining, and understanding relationships, ranging, for example, from
difficulties adjusting behavior to suit various social
contexts; to difficulties in sharing imaginative play or
in making friends; to absence of interest in peers.

This is another good example of how the DSM reasons from a
neurotypical point of view. Is not adapting to social circum-
stances an autistic problem? Or is it perhaps the polite, but
insincere behaviour of neurotypicals that we struggle with?
Isn't it actually very strange to lie when someone asks what
you think of their new shoes, or to keep acting nice to someone you really can't stand? Although *some* adaptability can
be a useful social lubricant, I think that if you adapt *too* easily, you aren't true to yourself.

My ex-boyfriend Mark was very good at adapting. He
had a work persona, a friend persona (the man's man who
makes jokes about 'chicks', drinks beer, and buys products
in blue-silver packaging), a family persona and yet another persona when he was around me. I always hoped that
that was his true self, but I couldn't be too sure. I remember
our first holiday abroad. This man, who was always so self-
conscious, suddenly turned into a dancing, frolicking come-
dian. Nothing wrong with that as such, of course, but it gave
me the fright of my life. I couldn't deal with it and so I asked

him to 'act normal'. He thought I was judging him because of his character, but that wasn't the case. I was just wondering, "Who are you and what did you do to Mark?!" "No one knows me here, so I can do whatever I want!" Mark, the somewhat locally famous TV personality, replied.

We had many discussions about it. "If I'm myself, people will think I'm a weirdo and I won't accomplish anything", was Mark's firm belief. I, on the other hand, had become convinced of quite the opposite over the years. "If you're yourself and people know about your crazy hobbies, the most amazing things will come your way!" I objected. I repeatedly dragged radio DJ and Disney fanatic Michiel Veenstra into this by his Mickey Mouse ears: If Michiel had kept his Disney obsession a secret for fear it would hurt his professional radio image, he wouldn't have become the voice of the announcements in Disneyland Paris and he wouldn't get invited to all kinds of cool press events. Plus, I can imagine his life is a lot more relaxed this way.

As a child, I didn't have much interest in my peers, but not because I didn't want to make contact. I simply had hardly anything in common with those kids. My high school was hell. Other kids single out an autistic classmate in no time, and this was no different in my case. I was a know-it-all of above average intelligence who was a year younger to boot. I had zero interest in boys. Zero interest in fashion. I still collected Pogs in my first year at high school.

In addition, my dislike of inaccuracies meant I have a hard time making friends. In that respect you could compare me to Bones, the character in the TV show of the same name – a forensic anthropologist who regularly offends colleagues with her blunt remarks. In one episode she refuses to acknowledge a colleague as a forensic foot expert, even when this hurts him so much it causes him psychosomatic problems. My ex-boyfriend Mark always thought Bones was annoying, but I can relate to her. Just like her, I have a very low tolerance for bullshit.

My yoga teacher once pulled out a small plastic battery-operated ball. "I will now demonstrate how powerful human energy is", she said prophetically. She asked us to sit in a circle and hold hands. Two people then touched the little ball, which closed the circle. A light went on. "Wow!" my fellow yoga students exclaimed. I didn't say anything, but in my head I was screaming, "We're just connecting a negative and a positive here, this is first-grade physics!"

You can't say things like that. Well, you can, but people won't like it. They will assume you think you're better than them, they will say you're arrogant. But putting my opinions aside, nodding along, smiling and keeping my mouth shut makes me feel uncomfortable, empty and angry. It sets off too many error alerts in my head, so I try to avoid such situations.

I still don't seem to click with most people, but by now, thanks to the internet (you know, that vilified medium where everyone is secretly a dirty old man), I have gathered a wonderful group of friends around me. Most are autistic or have similar traits. We share special interests, the same sense of humour and, most importantly: we can be ourselves. Always.

I have friends with whom I can sit on the couch in my sweats and don't need to say anything. To us, that's having a good time.

To everyone who feels they have to pretend to be something they're not and who is constantly afraid to step on people's toes I'd like to give this piece of advice: find better friends. You deserve it.

Behaviour and overstimulation

Where overstimulation finally got a mention in the DSM (somewhere in the back, preferably not in the title).

B Restricted, repetitive patterns of behavior, interests, or activities.

Echo! Echo!

1 Stereotyped or repetitive motor movements, use of objects, or speech (e.g., simple motor stereotypes, lining up toys or flipping objects, echolalia, idiosyncratic phrases).

Out of the second list of symptoms in the DSM-5, the list about behaviour, interests and overstimulation, you only need to have two to pass as autistic. In this first section I don't see much of myself: as far as I know I don't perform any repetitive movements and neither do I line up my stuff unnecessarily. Even the fidget spinner never did manage to captivate me.

Echolalia I do recognise: I too sometimes repeat sentences and words. I especially catch myself showing signs of delayed palilalia, repeating yourself hours after the conversation has passed. This usually happens while I'm doing the washing up or during another routine task. It's as if my head goes over all conversations that took place, re-examining them, and then emphasizing the little social cues ("Oh, yeah! No, sure! Cool!"). Out loud.

Other autistics I know benefit from *stimming*, certain repetitive movements or actions. Twirling, waving their hands, making ticking noises... Such things can be 'stims', things that soothe an autistic. I think stims put certain parts of the brain to work so that other, unpleasant stimuli can also be cleared away.

Stimming might seem odd, but if you think about it, you'll recognise stimming in a lot of neurotypical behaviours. Wiggling your legs, shaking your head or blinking when you see or hear something strange, making 'hmmm' sounds while eating, and even dancing – they're all actions where one part of the brain is stimulated in order to better process impulses from another sensory organ.

TIP

Question: What should I do when an autistic is stimming?
Answer: Nothing. Let them. Unless the autistic is hurting themselves or others, of course. In that case, try to direct the autistic towards another, less dangerous stim.

Rituals and patterns

2 Insistence on sameness, inflexible adherence to routines, or ritualized patterns of verbal or nonverbal behavior (e.g., extreme distress at small changes, difficulties with transitions, rigid thinking patterns, greeting rituals, need to take same route or eat same food every day).

Although Sheldon Cooper, the main character in the popular TV show *The Big Bang Theory*, doesn't have autism according to the writers (no doubt in order to avoid criticism, because an entire show based on laughing at someone with a developmental disorder wouldn't be very nice, of course), the fanbase isn't so sure. Even Jim Parsons, the actor playing Sheldon, says his character at least has autistic traits.

Sheldon leads his life according to a strict personal schedule; changes upset him. Every Monday morning he has oatmeal for breakfast and every Monday night, he and his friends order Thai takeout. Sheldon's order: mee krob and chicken satay with extra peanut sauce. Every Tuesday Sheldon has a barbecue bacon cheeseburger from The Cheesecake Factory, with bacon and cheese on the side. Wednesday night is Comic Book Night. Every Saturday night Sheldon does his laundry, at exactly eight fifteen.

It's one of the most common stereotypes: the rigid autistic who sticks to his schedule and freaks out over even the smallest changes. This is how many autistic characters in films or TV shows are portrayed. And that's not entirely wrong; a lot of autistics are like that, to a certain extent.

I too get agitated and stressed if I don't know what's going to happen, but especially when things are expected of me at the same time. I used to be a very picky eater for example, and had to know exactly at what time we were going to have lunch. Thinking about it now, it seems I mainly get anxious when I'm in danger of losing control. If we eat late, I get hungry and become particularly cranky. At some point it reaches a stage where I'm *so* hungry, I can't properly express what I want anymore – something I want to avoid at all cost.

When I'm travelling with someone else and I have the feeling I can't stop when I'm in danger of getting overstimulated, I get stressed. But if I can decide when I take a break, when I eat and at what time I go to bed, then I'll happily head out to Fukushima for a five-day trip without any plan whatsoever.

The need for structure is often misunderstood by outsiders, and even care workers. Ironically, they tend to interpret the need for structure a bit too literally, and they think everybody benefits from a daily schedule that's been planned to the max. The notion that people with autism might experience more stress due to a day that's been planned down to the hour (because the more that's been planned, the more that can go wrong) is lost on them.

TIP:
EXPECTATION MANAGEMENT

I once worked as a photographer at an event about autism, hosted by Kiehl's (the skincare brand). It appeared that the ladies who had organised the event had carefully studied the memo on how to deal with autistics: they went over the schedule with me in minute detail and kept asking if I had any questions. I regularly work as a photographer at events, so I thought their explanations were sweet, but a bit much. Suddenly, towards the end of the day, one of the ladies approached me: "Hey, ehm, we hadn't discussed this but ehm… could we get the photos by tomorrow?"
On the inside, I was laughing my head off. Luckily, I am not just used to events but also to overeager PR ladies, so I had already

blocked out the next day for photo selection and postproduction. But had I wanted to rest that next day, or had I already scheduled other work, my stress levels would have gone through the roof. Making such a last-minute request is exactly what you shouldn't do to autistics.

At a certain point, the autistic speakers started to become very restless: according to the schedule we were supposed to start at eleven o'clock, but by that time, all guests weren't even there. "It'll be at least eleven thirty, the same thing always happens at Fashion Week", I said casually, leaving the other autistics puzzled. I don't want to say I'm better at this, absolutely not. But I knew what to expect, and that makes all the difference.

If you're organising an event, conference, photoshoot or whatever with autistics, make sure to be clear. But be aware, too, that you shouldn't make promises you can't keep. A starting time of eleven o'clock may seem nice and clear, but in the aforementioned example it was way too specific. In a case like that, you're better off saying 'between eleven and twelve o'clock' (if that is feasible). That way, you'll avoid a lot of frustration. Of course we'd be even happier if the estimate would be 'between eleven and eleven O-five', but only if you can actually live up to it.

Trains vs. ponies

3 Highly restricted, fixated interests that are abnormal in intensity or focus (e.g., strong attachment to or preoccupation with unusual objects, excessively circumscribed or perseverative interests).

Most people are familiar with the stereotype of the autistic who loves computers, model trains or anime. But what about a preoccupation with horses, birds or linguistics? One of the reasons girls often get diagnosed late, is that parents and doctors don't perceive a girl who knows everything about horses as autistic. They mainly find it cute.

Ever since I had a relationship with someone who was a big fan of trains and theme parks, I know a thing or two about them myself. I already knew quite a bit about Disney parks, and it was because of this obsession that we met.

But why the obsessions? And why these specific subjects? Experts think predictability is a factor. Most autistic people's hobbies can be categorised or are logical or predictable. Horses or birds belong to animal species and have certain characteristics. Computers do what you tell them to do. (And if they don't, that's usually because you – or the software developer – made a mistake. A computer can't just go and decide to do something wrong because it doesn't like you, no matter how many people say it can.) Stamps can go into an album, bicycle race results can be compared. And sorting, categorising and calculating simply makes most autistics very happy.

I think the sense of happiness that autistics experience when they're immersed in their hobbies stems from the hyperactive circuits the Markrams talk about in their Intense World Theory. The stress we experience may be greater, but so is the payoff.

I can really get very excited about logic, good design or proverbial puzzle pieces falling into place. Positive stimuli, I call them. They 'click' in my head, thereby erasing other stimuli. The accompanying feeling reminds me of Tetris: the moment your blocks create a line you see a flash, the mess disappears and there is new room to build.

With some nice stimuli up ahead, we can overcome a lot of negative stimuli. I have an autistic nephew, for example, who'd normally never venture into a big crowd, but who overcomes all his sensory issues to meet his sports heroes during the local cycling event. It's exactly the same with my photography: the beautiful images outweigh the stimuli from contact, sun, wind and a lot of planning stress.

TIP

Support the autistic person in their quirky hobbies and obsessions; these are the moments they're at their happiest. Whether it's a K3 show or an afternoon of plane spotting, embrace it. Don't laugh at anyone, don't mock people. Don't say "You want to see that movie *again*?" or "You already *have* five hundred Star Wars figurines!", but look into it and find out what makes that one particular figurine so special. People who are as happy as a child when indulging in their hobbies, that's something I really love to see.

Stimuli

4 Hyper- or hyporeactivity to sensory input or unusual interest in sensory aspects of the environment (e.g., apparent indifference to pain/temperature, adverse response to specific sounds or textures, excessive smelling or touching of objects, visual fascination with lights or movement).

The issue autistic people have fought for for years has finally been added – as the very last symptom on list B of the DSM-5. The one thing which, to me and many others, is the most important aspect of our autism: hypo- and/or hypersensitivity to stimuli. It's the essence of the Intense World Theory and, in my opinion (and that of the Markrams), also the source of all additional problems.

All people experience stimuli. Sometimes many, sometimes few, sometimes consciously, but frequently completely subconsciously. Stimuli are the signals we receive mainly through the five senses, even though humans actually have more than five. And then there's the stimuli that come from your brain itself: thoughts.

A list of sensory stimuli

Sight

How do you recognise me? By that cap I always wear. A fashion statement? Sure, that too, but no, actually that cap is to keep the excessive amount of sunshine out of my eyes. If I forget my cap, I usually have a headache within a few hours. Sunglasses can be handy in such situations as well, but because I wear prescription glasses and don't feel like switching glasses all the time, I tend to stick to my cap. Plus, it helps to keep my hair out of my face, which can otherwise lead to both visual and tactile overstimulation.

There are places that, in terms of lighting, make me very unhappy as an autistic – the word 'hell' comes to mind. Take the convention centre in Utrecht for example. I really do enjoy strolling around the collectors' fair, but because of the halogen lamps hanging from the ceiling every meter, I can hardly see a thing. It creates multiple shadows coming off all objects which makes all depth disappear, my eyes can't focus anymore and my brain can't discern any details in the heap of information coming in through my eyes. After a couple of rows of stalls I start to get dizzy and want to get out as fast as I can.

Touch

Touch might be my most sensitive sense. I can't handle it very well if it's windy somewhere, if there's a draft or if the air conditioning is on full blast. That alone would make it impossible for me to work in an average office. Clothes are a challenge as well. Pants can't be too tight around my stomach, unless they're leggings with a broad elastic waistband of about eight centimetres or more – those are super comfy. Another autistic told me she has a pressure vest to help her calm down and I thought, "That's what I want!" I can't handle certain fabrics because they prevent my body from regulating its temperature. I get cold and hot at the same time as if I have a fever.

Touch can be just as intense in a positive way. A special person once told me, after driving me crazy by putting pressure on a certain spot on my lower back, that he was amazed at my sensitivity to touch.

But if I'm not in the mood, being touched is the most horrible thing in the world. So anybody who literally wants to give me a little push, as in "go on, your turn", or who puts an unexpected hand on my shoulder, can expect an imaginary punch.

Hearing

"Can we turn off the HRV?" I ask my boyfriend Riemer whenever I'm at his place. He has a new apartment in a tower in Rotterdam with a state-of-the-art ventilation system: Heat Recovery Ventilation. And it's gotta be turned off when I'm staying over, or I'll be overloaded in no time. It doesn't bother Riemer at all. Hotels are usually just as bad, if not worse. Most times their humming ventilation systems can't even be turned off.

Although the HRV doesn't bother him, Riemer is more likely to get overstimulated than I am in other ways. You can't have a conversation with him in a crowded restaurant, for example. All it takes is a group of prattling Pattys at the next table and the conversation is over. Filtering issues.

I can get really angry when my hearing gets overstimulated. I was once at the Europa-Park theme park with Mark when somewhere ahead of us in the queue (one of those boring zigzag queues where you keep shovelling past the same people) there was an annoying dude with a whistle. A whistle! The only thing worse are children's shoes kitted out with a squeaky rubber duck-type of noise (a Chinese invention to prevent your toddler from getting lost). I grew more and more angry at the shrill whistling noise, so when that dude passed me by for the umpteenth time, I punched him in the jaw – and it wasn't an imaginary punch.

Mark calmed the situation down and then said to me in a shocked and stern tone, "Will you never do that again? We could end up in a fight!" I promised him I'd never do it again, although I wasn't really sure I wouldn't: I hadn't *planned* to punch that dude, it just happened!

Smell and taste

Two senses that personally bother me less are smell and taste. Only cheap incense and cigars (regardless of how cheap they are) give me a headache, but I don't think that aversion is necessarily limited to people with autism. Other autistics say certain perfumes drive them crazy: "Chanel Chance truly ruins every date. It makes me nauseous", Lenny states on Twitter. "If a jumper has been washed with the wrong detergent, I take it off within three seconds!" another Twitter user writes. There are autistics who have difficulty shopping or travelling on public transport because of all the scents coming at them. Personally I draw the line at the perfume shop.

Due to their hypersensitivity to smells and flavours, a lot of autistic people struggle with eating. I too have had issues with food, even to the point of an eating disorder. And although I can be stimulated in a positive way by pleasant textures (marshmallows! liquorice!), I think my eating disorder mainly had to do with planning, choices and control. More about that later in this book.

Balance and proprioception

Besides the well-known five senses, people also have a sixth sense. And I'm not talking about the ability to see dead people, although I wouldn't mind Bruce Willis turning up beside my bed. The sixth sense on my list is proprioception, a system monitoring the position and location of your limbs. There's a seventh sense as well, by the way – balance. When stimuli related to proprioception and balance aren't processed properly, a person can trip, drop things or retain unnecessary tension.

Although generally, you can't tell by someone's looks whether they're autistic, I often recognise potential autistics by their posture. It's a bad posture, head forward, knees back and shoulders that are way too tense. The muscle tension throughout the whole body is very high, which makes these autistics look as if they're playing one of those zigzag games where you have to move a metal stick with a ring at the end along a wire without touching it. If you fail, you hear a ridiculously loud buzzer, get the fright of your life and don't win a hundred thousand dollars.

In my teens and twenties, I was that tense a lot of the time. My raised shoulders, shallow breathing and squinted eyes were a perfect recipe for headaches, which put me out of action for days. So upon recommendation of a friend, I started doing yoga a few years ago.

I had to get over the airy-fairy image, but consciously working with muscles and poses has enhanced my life significantly. I'm now quicker to notice when my muscles tense up. That helps me calm my breathing, and, in turn, my body and mind. In yoga, these three things are believed to be interconnected – which they are, of course. Your brain is a part of your body, and if you now decide to raise your left leg, you can. (Unless of course you're paralysed or don't have a left leg, in which case, sorry.)

Besides all the bending and stretching, yoga also includes some balance exercises that tap into your vestibular system (or your sense of balance). The beauty of balance exercises is that they immediately show you how your head and your other senses are doing. Do you have a busy mind and do other circuits keep demanding attention? Good luck trying to stand on one leg – it won't work. By consciously focussing on the balancing exercise, other parts of your brain start to calm down. After a while you get that "Psssht... Aaaaah!" sensation, like when you're opening a fresh bottle of Coke and release the pressure.

And you know what: I don't even like Coke. The carbonation in fizzy drinks is too much for my senses. By the way, did you know that the sound you hear when opening a bottle of Coke has been engineered? I bet those sound designers who worked hours to create the perfect *psssht* sound were at least bordering on autistic.

TIP

—

Imagine your own senses, multiplied by ten. A passing shopping trolley sounds like a low-flying fighter jet, a little breeze feels like an icy hand in your neck. Tight clothing becomes a metal harness you can't move around in and sunlight through the trees hits you like the flashing of a stroboscope you accidentally looked straight into.

I know autistics sometimes come across as terrible whiners. Drama queens. Crybabies. Even I think that sometimes, when another autistic complains about something that doesn't happen to affect me personally. But autistics aren't crybabies. They are people trapped in a world at volume 10. So close that window, turn down that music, and please don't force your child to wear itchy or polyester clothes. Give up that battle. Autistics will never 'learn to cope with it'. The only thing they will learn is to ignore their own body's signals. And that can be incredibly harmful.

Thoughts

"I have to get out of the loop. I have to get out of the loop." The sentence keeps repeating in my head, iron-ically turning into a loop itself. An hour ago I was at home, sitting on the white Malm cabinet that contains my clothes. I had gotten dressed, so that was a start. But after that I sat on that Malm cabinet, staring into space for minutes. "Go and do something, Toeps. Go outside. That always helps."

I wrote this passage on my blog two years ago. I felt over-whelmed by stimuli from within: thoughts. Thoughts that raced around my head like Formula 1 cars, lap after lap. Usually something like this happens the day after a busy workday with lots of communication. I'm tired, I'd love to just go to sleep, but at the same time my head just keeps racing. There's a schedule with a thousand things to be done and I'm way too hyper to go to sleep. But I'm tired. But I have things to do. But I'm tired. I get into a spiral I barely manage to get out of. Sometimes I grab my phone, only to conclude after a quick glance at Twitter that nothing new has happened in the past thirty seconds. Then the cycle starts again. I have things to do. But I'm tired.

By now I have developed a few good anti-loop-techniques. What works almost without fail is a change of scenery. In Tokyo I usually sit in a Starbucks where it's dead silent and people are working or studying. Sometimes I work, sometimes I stare at the screen of my laptop – that's when

I realise how run-down I really am. By now, I've also found a few nice spots in The Hague: Yoghurt Barn, the co-working space Collab at The Student Hotel and yes, even the communal living room at my apartment complex.

While writing this piece, it occurred to me I have gotten stuck in the loop a lot less over the past few months. My quieter, more flexible planning (more on this in part 5 of this book), my stable relationship with Riemer and my reliable emergency scenarios have given me a calmer state of mind than ever before. Hallelujah.

TIP:
TAKE CHARGE

Is an autistic you know stuck inside their own head? Maybe they don't mind if you take charge for a minute. "Will you come to Ikea with me? I need to pick up a rack." But do bear in mind that it's important not to burden the autistic with difficult questions or decisions. And definitely don't force anyone; to someone who is also auditorily overstimulated, Ikea would probably be the last place they'd want to go. I, on the other hand, usually love to go there.

When someone else is in charge, my head gets to take a well-earned break. My ex Mark would usually put on a TV interview or a documentary. If you'd asked me if I wanted to

watch it, I'd have said no. But because he was
watching, I'd start to get curious. And it didn't
matter if the topic didn't actually interest me.
It wasn't my decision. And that was wonderful.

Understimulation

Apart from overstimulation, understimulation is also common in autistic people. Some autistics, for example, barely
seem to feel pain or cold, ignore the urge to pee to the point
of it resulting in a bladder infection, or forget to eat or drink
for a whole day.

For me personally, this seems to happen because my
brain is busy doing other things at that moment – I often
forget to drink during photo shoots, for example, because I'll
be too busy taking photos. To prevent dehydration resulting
in a headache, I often ask my assistant to provide me with
something to drink every once in a while, and remind me to
actually drink it.

When I work from home, I often find it difficult to switch.
"Just this bit of code..." my brain mutters, after which three
hours have suddenly passed. What helps in such cases is a
schedule for the day with set breaks, setting an alarm clock,
or using a refillable water bottle that's always within reach.

Some people see stimming as a way to cope with understimulation, think of twirling or hand flapping. Pressure
vests and weighted blankets, or seeking out busy places like
a carnival, are also often mentioned as methods to battle

understimulation. I personally see it differently: I think they are ways to deal with overstimulation. That may not seem logical, but if you think back to the Tetris analogy from before: the stimuli caused by stims, physical sensations or crowded places seem to activate a clean-up system that, while processing these self-chosen stimuli, also clears away the unpleasant stimuli.

Executive functions

Problems with executive functions aren't explicitly mentioned in the DSM-5 as a symptom of autism, but I believe they're an essential part of the disorder. Executive functions oversee all kinds of processes in the brain, from self-control to executing complicated movements. People who have trouble with their executive functions struggle with dividing large tasks into smaller subtasks, separating important things from minor details and breaking patterns.

You might have noticed how remarkable it is that some brilliant autistics aren't able to cook, eat on time or keep their houses tidy. Other autistics stick to the rules of the systems they have created for themselves so strictly, that even the smallest change can really upset them. They're two sides to the same problem: trouble with executive functions.

A few years back, my household was a disaster as well. Laundry kept piling up in the bathroom, dirty dishes sat on the kitchen counter for days, and my desk was an ever-increasing collection of papers and items I needed to deal with. I was aware of the problem and I also knew what I needed to do to solve it: just start cleaning up! But the thought of 'just cleaning up' alone was enough to make my head explode.

Before my executive functions start to jam, a stream of thoughts and stimuli is set in motion that no amount of filtering can remedy. You could compare it to one of those machines that shoots out tennis balls, except that it's set to Serena Williams while I'm here having my first tennis lesson. With every tennis ball that zooms past me, the adrenaline rises. That's how it works when someone with autism wants to tidy up.

"This has to go into the closet!"

"But the closet still needs an extra shelf!"

"I should go get one at Ikea first!"

"Oh look, a dentist bill!"

"Better go and pay that first..."

Meanwhile sensory stimuli are all over the place, because there's clutter everywhere and everything feels unpleasant. Especially tasks like laundry or dishes – tasks that will get your hands wet or dirty – are tricky. The tornado of stimuli, or the mere prospect of it, can be so severe that the autistic person decides to do nothing – exactly like the Intense World Theory predicts. Dishes? Nope. Tidying? Nope. In my head, I see myself as a small child, covering my ears with my hands, shouting and stomping my feet. Nope, nope, nope! Brain overload.

It's weird, but my executive dysfunction doesn't seem as bad when other people are around. When I'm working, I seem to tap into a different source. This source is fuelled by stress hormones, by adrenaline, and the adrenaline enables my executive functions to work like a souped-up engine. That's not healthy, of course: where a souped-up engine overheats, my brain becomes exhausted and I get a headache. The next few days I get nothing done, unless I give myself an even bigger adrenaline boost. If you're not careful, this will lead to a downward spiral that eventually ends in panic attacks and symptoms of depression.

Thankfully there's a healthier way to deal with problems regarding executive functions. By dividing large tasks into smaller tasks according to a set system, a job like tidying up becomes a lot more comprehensible. I discovered declutter guru Marie Kondo's book, and it changed my life. I learnt to store things per category and to give each item its own assigned place. I learnt how to neatly organise my closets and cabinets and I found out that seventy-five per cent of the clutter on my desk could go straight in the bin. Because I follow the KonMari method, the fuzzy 'tidying up' has now turned into the much simpler 'putting things back where they belong'. And that I can do.

For other problems I have set the bar a little bit lower. When I'm in no state to cook, I eat a ready meal. Better than nothing at all. Because washing up is quite intense for me due to the sensory stimuli, I do my washing up under running water, rather than in a basin. I know it's more environmentally friendly to use a basin, but I have decided my functioning in this case is more important than holding on to my ideals.

TIP:
ELIMINATING BLOCKAGES

Do you ever think autistics are lazy and just need a kick up the arse? Chances are the person you're complaining about has trouble with their executive functions. To help them, you could set up a step-by-step plan. You could also try to find out what a possible blockage is about, and then offer to clear it away. For me it often is a huge ordeal to leave the house: I have to put on my shoes and jacket (stimuli!), it's cold (more stimuli!)... If this doesn't bother you as much as it does me, you could offer to go get me that one thing so I could just get on with my day.

I know some people will struggle with this because they feel like they're being used by a lazy autistic. And there are some lazy autistics out there, no doubt. But if you know which executive problems someone faces, you can take that into consideration.

Masking and the autistic burn-out

C Symptoms must be present in the early developmental period (but may not become fully manifest until social demands exceed limited capacities, or may be masked by learned strategies in later life).

Back to the DSM. We were at point C, a criterion I'd like to shout from the rooftops: symptoms are present from childhood, but it's entirely possible they don't manifest until the challenges in your life exceed your capacities and coping skills.

This is also referred to as the autistic burn-out: someone who was previously able to speak in coherent sentences, suddenly can't utter a single word or bursts into tears at the slightest change. It's the result of years of asking too much, of hiding and of "acting normal". The person in question shuts down and seems to become more autistic. But that's not the case: The person was always this autistic, they just ran out of energy to hide it.

It's the biggest danger in "high-functioning" autism. I use those quotes for a reason, because it's a subjective evaluation and all is not what it seems. Usually the person who seems to be functioning just fine, the one who appears to be doing well in society, is fighting to just keep their head above water.

How do you become a successful, functional autistic? Well, through social skills training, for example. When someone first suggested this to me when I was nineteen and in therapy for my eating disorder, I refused. I wasn't able to explain exactly why back then – learning social skills, that's supposed to be useful, right? But I felt that I'd never *really* be successful and that this training would only keep reinforcing my shortcomings. That every exercise would be torture and that I'd fail to get any *real* results. I will never feel comfortable looking people in the eye, for example. I still find that difficult. And the fact that I may do it more now, only means that on a daily basis, I spend more energy.

And that's where things start to go awry. Autistics who get better at learning how to "act normal" only end up spending more and more energy doing so. They get a normal job, yay, but in that job they have to keep up that act non-stop. They start a family, but constantly feel out of their depth. Three-two-one... Autistic burn-out.

Looking at my life, I can immediately point out at least five periods in which I had an autistic burn-out. I always thought I was just weak. A quitter. I quit three different studies, I had extreme difficulty looking after myself... And I didn't get it.

When I was diagnosed with autism, at first I thought I was going to learn how to cope with all my sensory overload. When that turned out not to be the case, I went through a mini mourning process. I now know how to avoid an autistic burn-out, but I still keep hitting my own limits – it's just that they always seem to be a bit closer than I'd hoped.

Significant limitations

D Symptoms cause clinically significant impairment in social, occupational, or other important areas of current functioning.

Oh right, keyboard heroes declaring on social media that "everyone's a little autistic" – nope. According to the DSM it has to really, *really* affect you. People with autism will miss days at work or have trouble with relationships, friends and family. They can't keep up in school because thirty kids with clicking pens and smelly deodorant drive them up the walls. They get kicked off the sports team because, according to them, something happened that wasn't in line with the rules (which was probably true, but the autistic in question just couldn't let it go). People who arrange their shoes by colour aren't "a little autistic", they're just shoe freaks.

It's not secretly something else

These disturbances are not better explained by intellectual disability (intellectual developmental disorder) or global developmental delay. Intellectual disability and autism spectrum disorder frequently co-occur; to make comorbid diagnoses of autism spectrum disorder and intellectual disability, social communication should be below that expected for general developmental level.

The last criterion is a sort of built-in fail-safe. It's only autism if it isn't anything else. Right.

Chapter 3

Let's get chronological

The Pink Tower and my parents' divorce

I was born thirty-four years ago. My mother was only twenty, my father twenty-four. Together they lived in a small flat in Zoetermeer that they got after living in my father's parents' attic for a while.

My parents were young and inexperienced, but at the same time that was their strength. They had no expectations and weren't bothered about the way things were supposed to be. I was their child, I was the one they looked at – not the neighbours' child. (And even if they had, our downstairs neighbours had a little boy who I think was at least as autistic as me, hahaha!)

I don't remember much about my early childhood. I know I used to hate certain socks, fancy socks with a lace trim and floral embroidery. I know I enjoyed the sound of the vacuum cleaner. My mother told me I taught myself how to read and that I'd get mad if the subtitles on TV were going too fast. We moved to a terraced house with a garden, I played with the boys next door, and all was well.

Until I started going to school. From the very first day, my behaviour went downhill. My mother still talks about the tantrums I had as soon as I got out of school. Everything came out: anger, vomit, poo, pee...

I don't recall much of that, but what I do remember vividly is feeling utterly misunderstood. "You're in your first year, so you can't write yet..." the teacher said one day. "I *can* write!" I shouted. "Not the way you're *supposed* to", the teacher said, "so you'll all get this printed label to stick onto the books you made." I was angry. Felt hurt, not seen. I didn't feel like doing any of it anymore. That stupid book. I stuck the label on upside down, because mentally I had already checked out and I didn't notice the book in front of me was lying the wrong way around. "Your label is on wrong, Bianca!" the teacher said, annoyed. "See, you can't read and write!"

Yeah, I get why I came home angry that day.

And then there was the situation with the dice. My classmates and I were sitting in a circle. The teacher pulled out one of those big, soft dice and every time someone rolled a six, they got to stack a wooden ring on top of a tower. That person was then praised by the teacher: "Good job, Dennis!" My toddler brain thought it was ridiculous. Although I lacked the words, it was all too clear to me that rolling the dice was pure chance, and that the student in question didn't deserve any compliments whatsoever.

When my behaviour got increasingly worse over the next few months, the school and my parents thought something had to be done. They decided to test my intelligence by giving me "the hardest puzzle in year two". It was a wooden puzzle on a board, with a busy picture. But to my surprise, a miniature version of the picture was drawn on the board itself! It seemed bizarre: how could this be the hardest puzzle in second grade if they gave away the solution from the start?! I finished the thing – for which I was given half an hour – in ten minutes. More time to play outside.

Okay, SOS, gifted child. Now what? My parents were put in touch with the local Montessori school.

I had a wonderful time at the Montessori school. It was heaven. They had materials such as the Pink Tower, which wasn't just their kindergarten's building tower but also the physical manifestation of exponentiation to the third power. (The Pink Tower is a tower with a bottom block of 10 by 10 by 10 centimetres on top of which sits a block of 9 by 9 by 9 centimetres, etcetera.) The shapes we would trace in the Montessori kindergarten turned out to be fractions and even Pythagoras' theorem was present, in the shape of a metal plate puzzle with a triangle in the middle and three squares bordering the triangle, filled with respectively 9, 16 and 25 squares of equal size. A squared plus B squared equals C squared.

I actually had a couple of friends at this school. Our downstairs neighbours' son also ended up at the Montessori school, a year above me. At recess we'd often talk about planets, or Russian letters. When I was a senior I hung out with Anneloes, a girl with hippie parents, who used to listen to ABBA in her room. I spent my lunch breaks with a group of kids building domino tracks that got longer and more advanced every day. At a certain point a computer arrived, one of those DOS things with green letters on the screen and big, flat floppy discs, on which I loved to play games. But even when the senior year students got to prepare a dance number to Ace Of Base's *The Sign* for the end-of-month celebration, led by the sexy Freya, a beautiful girl with long, black hair and olive skin who had clearly already hit puberty and wore such tiny shorts to school she might as well have worn nothing at all, I was allowed to participate. That was the Montessori school. A safe haven for everyone.

They would have liked to keep me there for another year. I had barely turned eleven when I had to start high school. I had skipped third grade, because as a second grader in my second/third grade composite class, I had already absorbed everything on the curriculum. During my senior year, I was solving math problems from a high school textbook. There simply was no way to keep me there. You probably wouldn't have been able to explain it to me.

While everything was going swimmingly in primary school, my parents got divorced. I was seven and one morning my mother was gone. She'd left a note saying she was going to stay with a friend. The next day she picked me up. I was playing with my train set in my playroom when I was told to come along. I don't think I even got the chance to tidy up.

It was a strange time. My mother and I moved in with the aforementioned friend. She herself had a husband and three children, but they cleared a room in their large terraced house that my mother and I shared. At first my father used to come by in the evenings to wish me good night. But saying goodbye every night was *so* hard on me, that they decided not to do that anymore. To this day I feel guilty about that towards my dad.

What followed was the mother of all nasty breakups. One lawsuit after another about money. Two different sets of house rules. A new boyfriend for my mother, and a new girlfriend for my father. My mother's boyfriend was violent and addicted to alcohol. The atmosphere at home was grim, so when I was about eight years old I moved from my mother's to my father's house. My mother wasn't happy with the way things were going and let me read all the letters from lawyers, even though I was only a child. One day I took my bike and rode away angrily, and didn't want to see her for months.

That was when both my parents, separately, alerted several authorities. I was seen by social workers, but without much continuity: one got sick, another left, a third one retired. On top of that, I didn't trust them anyway. They said they weren't going to say anything to my parents, but I didn't believe that for one minute. So everything was going just fine, thanks, and that was that. Did they think I was autistic? No. Highly intelligent, yes. But I think that had as much to do with the zeitgeist as with anything else. Giftedness was the hot new thing, and if that meant you weren't as social, oh well. That was just part of it.

From first grade to Disneyland

I had just turned eleven when, for my first day at high school, I arrived at the scene wearing shorts, a white T-shirt emblazoned with the Ajax football club logo, a Super Mario bum bag containing Pogs and the same hairdo as Backstreet Boy Nick Carter. Some kids were wondering whether I was a boy or a girl.

Contrary to the Montessori school, at Alfrink College, they graded us. I was deeply disappointed when I only scored a 9 out of 10 at an English test, because I had written 'gril' instead of 'girl'. And not just disappointed: I was mortified by this capital mistake. It could never happen again.

I became the class egghead, the kid who always got good grades. My classmates thought I was weird. The most painful affirmation of this was the time I was leafing through Trishna's school diary, probably looking for cutouts of Leonardo DiCaprio, when a contribution by good girls Esther and Claudia caught my eye: "Oh, poor Trishna! So sorry you have to sit next to 'it'!" It. That was me. I also remember the time in economics when I was laughing because Christine had added costs to her profit. I thought it was a beautiful example of creative bookkeeping, but Christine saw it as a personal attack. "Are you laughing at me?!" I wasn't laughing at her; I thought her mistake was funny. A completely different thing in my eyes.

I still cringe when I think back to that music class where I recited a rap song while wearing a retainer. I was only allowed to take out my retainer during recess to eat. So when our music teacher asked us to write raps, after which he played the recording back for the whole class room, all you heard in my case was a disgusting, lisping saliva symphony. Another moment that still haunts me is that time in Mr Kooijman's class when I tried to imitate a joke from Donald Duck magazine, where you get someone to stick their nose in a book and then slam it shut in their face. Very funny when you do it to Neighbour Jones, not so effective in real life. Mr Kooijman yelled "Ouch!" and was mainly angry. I was such a dork.

Not just my behaviour was peculiar, so was my sense of fashion. There were strict rules at my father and stepmother's house; I had to return purchases made with my allowance several times because they did not pass inspection. One of those Adidas pants with buttons on the side. A camo print shirt. Skater pants. When I bought the Airwalk trainers I so desperately wanted, I decided to wear them right away. That way they couldn't be returned, at least. I was punished of course, but it was worth it.

At my mother's I could wear whatever I wanted. Baggy pants with camo print combined with a crop top or a bodysuit. Name-brand jumpers that were undoubtedly fake knockoffs, bought at some shady dealer. It must have been incomprehensible for my classmates: one day I'd wear a sweet jumper with a teddy bear print, the next day I was a Spice Girl.

The difference in rules didn't just apply to clothing. While my mother mostly let me go about my business, my father and stepmother attempted to bring structure by micromanaging. For years, there was a giant list of house rules on my closet door, describing in detail how I should wash myself, dress myself, wipe my bum and tidy my room. As far as I remember, I was doing a pretty decent job at doing those things myself, but apparently they did notice something was up with me. You might think a list like that would be handy for children with autism (even though I didn't have that diagnosis yet back then), but to me, it was mainly terrifying. Because what if, according to the list, you're supposed to wipe your bum three times, but the toilet paper is already clean after two wipes?

Another thing was that, according to the rules, there were only two pairs of shoes allowed in the hallway. But what if there were guests? Or if the floor had just been mopped? Then the shoes had to be on the mat, but as soon as the floor was dry that was out of the question... I got confused and started doing silly things. Irrational things. You know, like in a multiple-choice test where you change your answer to A at the very last second, while you *knew* it was B.

There were times when tension reached such a fever pitch that I ran away to my mother. By that time she had dumped the drunk loser and met a nice new boyfriend. But every time I reluctantly returned to my dad because I felt I would hurt him terribly by moving away permanently. My mother always let me make up my own mind. Thinking back to it, my heart aches. Of course she would have loved for me to stay with her. But somehow I knew: my mother can handle it if I leave. My father can't.

Eventually it was my dad himself who, when I was thirteen, decided I should go live with my mother. It had been used before as a threat, just like the 'home for problem children', but this time it wasn't a threat; it was a solution. "She's getting more and more withdrawn, I'm afraid she's going to hurt herself", my father said to my mother in a rare and serious phone conversation.

I moved. A few weeks later my old bedroom had been turned into an office and my football and basketball, which had been gifts from my aunt and uncle, had the name 'Mitchell' written on them in black marker. Few things have ever hurt me more.

Nothing to do with Mitchell – Mitchell is my half-brother and I wish him nothing but the best. He's ten years younger than me, and he's my father and my stepmother's child. I didn't know what to expect with a new baby, but it turned out to be the best thing ever. I taught him how to read, built DUPLO, LEGO and K'NEX towers with him, understood his baby talk, and best of all: he totally accepted me. Whenever I was being punished, he'd come up to me and say: "No cry, Bianta!"

But seeing his name on my toys hurt, because it felt like I was being kicked out of the family. Exit Bianca, or at least it seemed that way. The bond with my brother was hanging by a thread as well. For the longest time, I was afraid to tell my parents how hurt I was for fear of being misunderstood and provoking a fight. I knew what the result would be: no more contact with the little four-year-old rascal. He'd forget me. I would cease to exist.

In the years that followed, I became obsessed with everything my brother liked. *Pokémon* (the cards as well as *Pokémon Gold* and *Silver* on the Gameboy), *Rollercoaster Tycoon*. I cherished the memories of our family trip to Disneyland Paris and learnt everything about the parks. After we saw the film 'Abeltje' in the cinema, I spent hours listening to its theme song, 'Vlieg met me mee' (*Come fly with me*). I still well up when I suddenly hear that song somewhere.

Disneyland has always remained important to me. So much so that at age fifteen, I travelled to Disneyland Paris together with my best friend Reema.

Reema and I were in the same class in third grade. People immediately warned her about me: "She's weird!" But Reema was one of those girls who didn't care about other people's opinions. She wanted to see for herself just how weird I really was. We used to cycle home together, and if we weren't hanging out in town, we'd be in her room. One day, we made a plan. "If we save up a hundred *guilders* every month... we can go to Disneyland Paris next year!"

And so we did. We picked tomatoes at a local greenhouse over summer. My mother was proud: "My daughter is saving up!" I learnt one of the most valuable life lessons ever: you can achieve a lot if you make a plan and go for it. After saving up for a year, Reema and I got onto a coach and headed for Disney.

That year wasn't just one big party though – I was at home almost half the time. My mother wasn't aware at all; after

I'd moved from my father's to my mother's house, school lost track. They didn't know who to go to anymore and in the confusion that followed, I took it upon myself to provide them with my mother's new signature. That way I could sign my own absentee notes. My mother once commented she thought the school's communication was very lax. Oh, she didn't know half of it.

I stayed home because I simply couldn't cope anymore at school. The bullying, the feeling of not being accepted, the constant adjusting and masking... I was tired, dead tired. On top of that I was working after school. At first at the local supermarket, then at a fast food joint. Jobs that weren't suitable for me at all, but my mother thought it was a good idea – it would make me more sociable.

Of course I didn't become more sociable. I'd usually head to work shaking with anxiety, even though it was only for a few hours. The supermarket was the worst: I went to work, hoping that nobody would ask me anything in the two hours it took me to clean the staff room. I would avoid the shop floor at any cost; what if someone wanted to know where to find the potatoes while I was on my way to the aisle with cleaning products for a bottle of bleach! I'd rather scrub the toilets for two hours straight.

All together it was too much. Too demanding. Too over-whelming. So I stayed home during the day, ate all the cook-ies in the pantry and watched the *Travel Channel* all day long. (If it happened to be about Disneyland Paris, I would easily stay home all week.) I'd sneak out to the supermarket in the afternoon to buy a new box of cookies and put it in the pantry to replace the box I'd devoured. By the time my mother got home, I was about to head out to my fast food job. As far as she was concerned, I'd been in school all day.

My grades took a dive, but luckily I was smart enough to make sure they didn't plummet too far. My father, however, did notice the drop, and he complained, "You'll never amount to anything this way!" My final year arrived, and I decided to make a change. Those final grades are *forever*, so I had to get them up. No matter what.

It worked. I spent a little less time at my job, and more time studying. Plus I started going back to school on a daily basis. The bullying seemed to have gotten less, and there was a group of students I kind of connected with. A bit like a third wheel, but I was like, I'll take it. And yet I needed something. Something to get me through the days. My secret weapon became… Sugar.

To a certain extent, it had always been my medicine, a way to boost myself both physically and mentally. During the time at my father's, when he kept close track of my pocket money, I would make up library penalties. With that money, I'd buy marzipan. Of course I'd get a lecture about the penalty, but that was totally worth it.

In my senior year, sugar became my drug. I needed it to push past my own boundaries, to push myself to go to school, to push myself to go to work, to motivate myself, to reward myself… It gave me headaches and made me sick, but I ignored that. It helped me perform. I graduated almost top of my class.

Toeps the accountant

I knew I didn't want to study. At least not immediately. During an orientation day at Erasmus University everything in my head was screaming 'no' – this was too big, too intense, too complicated. And besides, what should I study?

At the college fair in third grade I knew exactly which study programmes interested me. Japanology. Or fashion. Art school perhaps, or industrial design. But when I came home with the brochures, they didn't get a very warm reception: "Japanology? What do you need *that* for?" Everything less than university was automatically earmarked as a sub-par option. Why else did I finish high school at top level? It was best to pick a 'smart' option, one that would make me rich. Economics, or something like that. I couldn't see myself doing that. So I didn't.

I opted for a gap year. I secretly dreamt of a job at Disneyland Paris, but at seventeen, I was too young. I went to a temp agency for an administrative job instead.

After a few detours I ended up in the accounting department of a large engineering company. My first job was to check the receipts in the expense reports filed by engineers after their business trips. The work was fun: nosing around in other people's receipts, often from far-away countries. The differences between the engineers were fascinating: one would have a plain sandwich, the other would spend hundreds of euros at restaurants while even claiming the fifty cents he'd had to pay to use the bathroom. I neatly processed the reports in a computer system and the corresponding Excel sheet. And because I was at it anyway, I improved that sheet by adding equations and proof calculations. My supervisor was happy with my work and soon gave me more responsibilities.

It was the best workplace I could ever have ended up: not only did I enjoy the work, my colleagues were lovely as well. They were the ones who took me to the cafeteria every lunch break and made sure I ate well. They were the ones who donated their old furniture to me when I left home at the tender age of seventeen. And they were also the ones who one day put a full-page ad on my desk: *The Tax Office is looking for top-level high school graduates to be trained as audit specialists.*

I left home because I started living together with my then-boyfriend, a former classmate I'll call Wiebe. After camping out in his bedroom in Zoetermeer for a few months, I decided to move with him to The Hague. I was seventeen. Which leads to some interesting situations, by the way – if you want to get cable, for example, but you're not allowed to sign the contract because you're, oh right, underaged.

I was making enough money to support myself, but the pressure to finally study Economics with a capital E still lingered. Nearly a year had passed, the new academic year was about to start – in short, time was running out. And that's when my colleagues showed up with that Tax Office ad.

A dual study programme over seven years that would train me to become an accountant/audit specialist. It came with a permanent contract, a good salary, *and* the entire study programme at Nyenrode Business University was paid for. I actually wanted to go to Disneyland, but hey, Wiebe wouldn't appreciate that, my dad wouldn't appreciate that, and oh well, auditing... That's basically what I was doing in my current job, wasn't it? It was kind of fun. So I applied for the role. I scored extremely high on the IQ test, but pretty poorly on the stress resistance test. That really stressed me out, but I was hired after all.

Together with Wiebe's mum, I went to H&M for some sharp shirts and a pinstripe two-piece suit. Suddenly I was ten years older than I am now. Three days a week I went to class in Breukelen, at an estate with a castle and ostriches, where I was part of the Tax Office class together with 27 other lucky students. And I was good – many times even the best, or at least in the top 3. To me it kind of felt like I had to; I knew I probably wasn't the most sociable person, but this was a way to compensate for that.

Despite my social ineptitude, in this class, I suddenly belonged to the popular group. That is to say – I was allowed to join them on trips. We went out for dinner, went skiing, there was drinking and half the class was sleeping around with each other. Apparently that lifestyle comes with the territory, even in this nerdy class without the big fancy cars, that the frat boys at KPMG and PWC made fun of.

And everybody bought a house. We were able to because we had permanent contracts, and because the 2008 financial crisis was still six years away. So by the time I was eighteen, I had a house with a mortgage, a boyfriend, a dog and a job for life. Or so it seemed.

While things were going well at uni (partly because we were at Nyenrode on Mondays, Wednesdays and Fridays, and Tuesdays and Thursdays were dedicated to self-study, or recovering), I was having a hard time at the internships. During those periods, we didn't have class, but worked full time at the Tax Office instead. Those periods were a disaster.

The first internship wasn't too bad. I was doing VITA, or Volunteer Income Tax Assistance. Every 30 minutes, a different taxpayer sat down at my desk, often with a shoebox full of receipts and other potential deductibles and no idea what they were doing. I loved helping people, using everything I knew about the law to assist the person sitting across from me as well as I could. I clearly remember the immigrant woman in front of me, recently divorced and more or less escaped from a repressive marriage. This woman was so strong and brave, and she told me she had started a driving school for women because there was a demand for that in her community. It never occurred to her that those costs were deductible. But because we spoke about it, I was able to file her tax return in such a way that she didn't have to pay anything. It makes me smile to this day.

But it wasn't all fun and games. I would often get into arguments with a supervisor about the interpretation of certain pieces of legislation. And although I was probably right, I didn't realise that arguing in front of a room full of taxpayers was pretty unprofessional. A note was made on my internship report. I thought that was unfair – I was right, wasn't I?!

I absolutely hated the second and third internships. They were auditing internships, and during the company visits and audits I discovered that reality was very different from the theory I had been taught in class. I wanted to monitor the rules, but my mentors and the counterparty's accountants were mainly bickering about the value of pension plans or work in progress. These kinds of arguments could take months, sometimes years, and usually ended up being settled in court.

During my third internship I was expected to write letters and call taxpayers myself. I was terrified. I had never liked making phone calls in my previous jobs, but calling on behalf of the Tax Office – the bad guy – was even worse. I was too scared to do it. So I didn't. I spent my entire third internship staring at files, sitting on the toilet, eating cake at colleagues' birthdays, taking two-hour lunch breaks, and staring at some more files for good measure. On top of that, I called in sick for two weeks – the maximum period before having to redo the entire internship.

It was during this time that my sugar addiction got completely out of control.

The eating disorder era

My eating habits had always been a bit odd, but during my time at Nyenrode they went from bad to worse. I needed more and more sugary treats to get through the days. Dutch liquorice coins, because I love the way they slide in my mouth, and a bag of them can last up to half a day. Marshmallows, because they're so wonderfully soft. Ice cream. And during the holiday season: marzipan.

Candy motivated me, but it had two huge downsides: 1) it makes you fat, and 2) it makes you sick. And if you start skipping meals because you don't want to get fat, you get even sicker.

The scale became my latest obsession. I knew my mother weighed 63 kilos, so that's what I wanted to weigh as well. Measuring 1.83 metres makes me five centimetres taller than my mother but hey, better safe than sorry. I went from 70 kilos to 67, to 65 and 63, and then to 60 because that gave me a bit of margin. How did I do that? Simply by not eating. If I felt I had wolfed down too much candy during the day, I would skip dinner. That way I kept the numbers under control. My health, on the other hand, was rapidly declining.

I would regularly (nearly) faint and my blood sugar was doing weird things. I blamed it on hypoglycaemia and started following the Atkins diet. I traded in my bags of liquorice for tubs of mascarpone (which I ate straight out of the container), but I couldn't keep it up. After all, my food binges were meant to help me get through my day, and mascarpone didn't do that nearly as well as the massive sugar rush I got from ice cream, liquorice or marshmallows.

But at some point, even that wasn't enough anymore. I started throwing up, couldn't motivate myself anymore with a single bag of candy and my seemingly perfect life started showing cracks. I missed classes because I was at home with a headache, Ben & Jerry's, and panic attacks. The Tax Office sent me to a psychologist, but that didn't help either. I was exhausted. But because I didn't recognise what was happening, I convinced myself my job was the issue, and I resigned. I got a job on the side and collapsed again two weeks into that. It wasn't until then that I decided I needed some serious help.

I ended up at *De Ursula*, an institution specialised in eating disorders. I was in therapy three days a week, both in a group and individually. The therapy gave structure to my weeks, and in the eight months I spent there, I was able to pretty much reconstruct my whole life.

My relationship with Wiebe ended, I sold him my share of the house and moved into a pink studio apartment by myself. Subsequently, my eating disorder quickly improved. I learnt why I ate, learnt to recognise my triggers and created structure. However, in hindsight I do blame *De Ursula* for one thing: not picking up on my autism.

I recently came across a box of old papers while moving house. In it, among other things, was my treatment plan. The first goal I defined, of course, was 'to eat better'. The second goal? 'To work on social anxiety'.

By now scientific research has shown that an autism diagnosis is relatively common in people suffering from the eating disorder anorexia nervosa.[9] I had an eating disorder NOS (not otherwise specified), but that doesn't change my point: they should have been more alert.

I've often wondered why I had this eating disorder. I think there were multiple factors at play. Sensitivity to stimuli is one of them; there still are plenty of foods I don't like to eat, because they feel unpleasant. At the same time, my sensitivity to pleasant stimuli meant certain foods helped me get through the day.

Structure is another factor. You need to eat at least three times a day, but you can't eat the same thing every day. All that planning, decision making, grocery shopping and preparing causes many autistics a lot of stress.

It actually makes sense that autistics seek solace in food. The brain needs sugar to function. And my brain, with its amped up, hyper-connective circuits the Markrams talked about in their Intense World Theory, probably uses a lot of it. I just didn't have the capacity to fulfill that need in a responsible manner at the time.

---

9 Anckarsäter, H., Hofvander, B., Billstedt, E., Gillberg, I., Gillberg, C., Wentz, E., & Råstam, M. (2012). The sociocommunicative deficit subgroup in anorexia nervosa: Autism spectrum disorders and neurocognition in a community-based, longitudinal study. Psychological Medicine, 42(9), 1957-1967. DOI: 10.1017/S0033291711002881

I believe the flip side of this effect applies to people suffering from anorexia nervosa, who *barely* eat. After a period of hunger, a person who barely eats enters a sort of numb, floating state. People in the group who suffered from anorexia told me that the biggest problem with eating more was that it made them feel more. Sensory overload.

Speaking of sensory issues: tight clothing, or actually all fabric touching my stomach, still causes me to reach sensory overload super fast. I used to think a flat stomach would solve this problem: when your clothes rest on your hip bones, you don't feel them rubbing up against you every time you breathe or move. By now I have a wardrobe full of loose-fitting pants, stretchy leggings and jumpers and shirts that can best be described as "tents". You'll never get me into a two-piece suit again.

Take two

De Ursula marked the second beginning of my life. I learnt to listen to myself, started to get a sense of my boundaries and limitations and did things I liked. I'd often go on weekend trips to Disneyland Paris, my obsession at the time. I met a nice new boyfriend, the amusement park enthusiast and fellow autistic who, from here on, shall be referred to as Arnout. I started the blog I still write to this day. I did a photoshoot, as a model, for a group of amateur photographers I met on an online forum. I signed up with a casting agency as an extra, thanks to which you would have seen me in the background of several TV ads – well, if you didn't happen to blink that very second, that is.

The course I decided to enroll in at the university of applied sciences, Communication and Multimedia Design, complemented all of that. I learnt about websites, photography, usability, graphic design and marketing. And yet, I didn't finish the course. I dropped out in my second year, after a group assignment that went particularly wrong.

Group assignments: the second favourite pastime for people who are into self-chastising. It's not just autistics, by the way, who have difficulty working as a group; most non-autistics I know hate it as well, although the consequences might be a little less severe for them. "Yeah, but", teachers say, "out there in the *real* world, you'll have to work together as well!" By now I have more than ten years of experience in the real world, and I can tell you: that's bullshit. Yes, as a photographer, I work with other people. And no, that doesn't always go smoothly. But do I ever work with the stoned, perpetually late losers who were in my class? No, of course not. As someone who is self-employed I get to pick and choose who I work with, and I simply refuse projects where I'd be working with useless slackers.

As a student, you can't. And so you always end up in one of two nightmare scenarios: you either do the whole project yourself, or you fail because the two numbnuts you're stuck with didn't do their work. The latter happened to me in my second year. That failed grade meant two things: doing another project in a different group where I didn't know anyone at all, and delaying my course. Once again I refused to admit I wouldn't be able to cope with that, so once again I convinced myself I wanted to do something else. I enrolled in art school to do photography.

It was an impulsive decision, and I could have saved myself a lot of grief if I'd taken more time to compare academies, but I was just happy to be accepted to *St. Joost* in the city of Breda. I said goodbye to CMD and started making some money shooting portraits in the meantime.

I didn't like art school at all. Too vague and artsy. I wanted to be a fashion photographer, but the teachers at *St. Joost* thought that was shallow and one-dimensional. We were making Art with a capital A. Because I wasn't exactly waiting for a life of grant writing, exhibitions, and PR pitches about the meaning of my work, I decided art school wasn't for me. Thankfully, I had quite a bit of freelance work by then.

A conversation with my father

"You're not one to let things get you down", my dad said to me recently. It wasn't until later that I realised how much this comment meant to me; I've always been afraid he'd see me as a quitter, as someone who never finishes anything.

I decided I wanted to speak to my father after our first conversation about this book.

"Autism isn't an excuse for everything", he said firmly. I wondered what exactly it was that it wasn't an excuse for. I also wondered why he reacted so belligerently. It almost seemed as if this wasn't about me, but about something bigger.

A few weeks later he visited me at my office. I had written down my questions and had been extremely nervous all day. I took half an Imodium tablet and half an oxazepam – a recipe that would surely result in me being violently ill two days later, but hey, at least I'd be able to function that evening. My dad had bought me a Spyder for my birthday, a little device to properly configure the colour tones on a screen. "It's the Express, but if you look up a license online, you can also use it as the Pro. It's the same device!" That's the kind of stuff my dad knows.

I was nervous, because our relationship hadn't always been the best. We had reconnected a few years ago, and I wanted to keep it that way. I looked at my sheet of paper, but before I could even say anything, my dad started talking.

"Look, we didn't know, of course." That sentence would come up again and again in this conversation. My father and stepmother had no reason to assume I was autistic, so they had tried to find other explanations for my behaviour. Rebellious adolescent behaviour. The result of the divorce. Maybe partly my mother's fault as well, as she was apparently trying to undermine the authority in the Dad Residence.

"Although I don't really want to go into all that", my father said. He generalised: "It was a difficult situation for us."

I get him though.

Without having seen my list of questions or earlier drafts of this book, he started talking about the shoes in the hallway. How they always used to be an obstacle. "We were strict, but we were clear, right?" I'm glad I finally got to explain to my dad how confusing the shoe rules had been to me. For the second time, I felt like my father and I had come a little closer together.

A few weeks earlier we had a moment like that as well.

"Can you handle criticism?" my dad had asked during a lunch date. It was July, and ever since February I'd had the feeling I had done something wrong. Now finally, the truth would come out. "You're very self-absorbed", my dad said.

This is how he came to that conclusion: in February, just as I was about to leave for Japan for three months, we ate together. My father, stepmother, my boyfriend Riemer and I. While enjoying a pizza I was talking about my travel plans. "...and then in May Mitchell and Lianne are coming over..." Mitchell, my little brother, was off travelling the world together with his girlfriend Lianne. After a period in Vietnam and a trip across Australia and New Zealand, they'd come over to Japan, and I was going to visit Disneyland Tokyo with my brother. It was supposed to be a poetic happy end to a period of fear, a confirmation our bond was restored once and for all. While planning my Japan trip I had always made our visit to Disneyland Tokyo my number one priority. Even a big work project had had to make way for it.

"Well, I wouldn't count on it!" my stepmother said.

My dream was shattered.

"What? Why not?"

"Well, Mitchell called yesterday… They're breaking up. They're coming home this weekend."

I felt tears welling up. I looked at Riemer, who knew what this news meant to me. I mumbled something about 'my planning'. My dad took this as an extremely selfish act. It wasn't until I explained the reason for my crying months later, that he understood.

"Do you think you also have autism?" It's the scariest question on my list. Most kids find out at a certain age that their parents aren't the infallible superheroes they once seemed. But that my father might be autistic as well? It had never occured to me. Family members had joked about it. When he visited me at my place a little while later and went on and on about the type of lift in my building, the pennies started dropping like the little balls in a pachinko machine.

"I sometimes suspect I might, a little…" My father talks about his preference for structure. About wanting things in just the right spot at home. About that time he got pretty angry at my stepmother when she changed the interior of the bathroom. "She could have at least discussed it with me!"

"And you also have some issues with sound, right?" I ask. I remember something about a high-pitched sound coming from the TV.

"Definitely!" my dad says. He lists: "Kids playing outside with a ball, a rattle in the car..." There are more examples than I'd expected.

"And do you think grandpa was autistic too?" To me, this was actually an open-and-shut case. My grandfather wanted to go on holiday to the same campsite every year, and it always had to be cabin number 47. He ate the same thing every day. Every week on Sunday we'd get Chinese takeout. My grandfather was a programmer at a time when computers still had green screens, and in his spare time he would do logic puzzles: the ones where Mary has a red car but doesn't live at number 7, from which you should be able to deduct that the person at number 8 has a brown dog.

My dad mutters, "Grandpa? No..."

I'm so surprised that I cry out, "No?" I go over the list above.

My dad hesitates and thinks out loud: "Right, well... You *could* see things like that as characteristics of someone on the autistic spectrum."

It seems like he'd just never thought about it that way. And I get that. To my father, grandpa is just his dad.

So I don't let things get me down, according to my dad. Most of the time, I didn't really have a choice: a person has to eat, and I wasn't on social benefits or had a partner with a money tree.

"And that's a good thing", I tell my dad, "because with social benefits as a safety net, I probably never would have challenged myself." He agrees with me. He wonders to what extent some people use their autism as an excuse to never try anything new or exciting. Aha, I think, *that's* what he meant.

Immediately I add some nuance: it's not healthy to push people so far that they end up with a burn-out either. I also think of my ex Arnout, who was on social benefits since he was eighteen, but bid the welfare office farewell after our break-up to go work in an amusement park abroad. He didn't speak the language and had zero experience, but ten years later, he's still there. Is he an exception to the rule?

The next day I tell my friend Veerle about the conversation with my father and repeat my mantra: "I never would have gotten this far if I'd been on social welfare."

"I don't believe that at all", Veerle objects. "You're always busy doing something, you never would have just stayed at home. You would have found something else, or built something step by step."

Shit. Maybe she's right. Maybe I've been telling myself all this time it's a good thing I struggled like I did – as if that's the reason I've achieved things. I'm happy with where I am now, but maybe I would have gotten here via a different route as well. I think back to the brochures I'd gathered in my third year of high school. Japanology. Fashion. Design. Five minutes earlier I had been telling Veerle about the webshop I was working on. We also spoke about my Japan trips, and my work as a photographer. It's clear: I'm exactly where I'm supposed to be. And I probably would have gotten there no matter what.

I look back on the conversation with my father with a sense of satisfaction. Apart from the fact that I feel seen, I also see *him*. I now have a better understanding of how hard it must have been for him, back then. The pain of the divorce, the difficulties he and his new wife had to deal with. I started this conversation because I felt it could be interesting for my book, but I eventually got much more out of it: a strengthening of our bond.

Toeps the fashion photographer

My love for photography started on the other side of the camera: as a model. Not that I was some sort of top model, absolutely not. My biggest accomplishment as a model was a photoshoot for Holland Casino. (That picture is still displayed at Schiphol airport. Check it out next time you enter the Netherlands: that's me hanging on the wall, lurking over a roulette table, welcoming you.) Apart from that, I did a bunch of terribly ugly photoshoots or acted as an indistinct blur in the background of a TV ad.

But for me it wasn't about getting my fifteen minutes of fame, although I can't deny I loved seeing myself on TV for the first time. What mainly intrigued me was the process of creating something out of nothing. I also noticed I was better at social situations if they came with a script and were rehearsed beforehand. I've always had a thing for fake worlds. Disneyland of course is one big show, and places like Las Vegas and Dubai intrigue me as well because of all the façade. It seemed to confirm the feeling I've had deep down all along; that our world consists of a collection of veneers that peel away in places, allowing us to peek underneath the surface.

I wanted to work in that world. Create fantastical images of my own. So I became a photographer. I signed up to several different forums where I found models, makeup artists and stylists to work with. I also regularly posted work on my blog. I earnt money by photographing people; mostly extras just like me, who needed new photos for casting agencies every once in a while.

Getting connected in the world of photography was relatively easy as I had something to offer: good photos. So many people suddenly wanted to be my friend that I had to learn to differentiate: who's here for me, and who's only my bff to take advantage of me?

Modelling agencies especially had a habit of doing that. They're forever looking for willing photographers to photograph their 'new faces': fourteen-year-olds fresh off the street who might be pretty, but are usually extremely inexperienced, which made shoots with them a huge gamble: will this result in anything usable at all? A modelling agent once invited me over to her home and showered me with *so* many compliments, that I just started staring into space, thinking: "This woman isn't all there."

But on the flipside, I also met photographer Ruud and model Maan, both of them still good friends ten years later. Maan participated in Holland's Next Top Model, the exceptionally unrealistic modelling show I enjoy watching to this day, if only to bash every single thing about the show. Actually, that's exactly what I was doing when I wrote about Maan on a forum. Not that I was bashing *her*, on the contrary. Maan was presented as a clumsy girl who just couldn't seem to get a good picture. I came across some photos by Ruud, who had worked with Maan before the TV recordings. The photos were gorgeous. And that's what I posted on the forum.

Ruud noticed that his website suddenly got a lot of views and started to investigate. He found my forum post, clicked through to my blog and sent me an email asking if he could photograph me one time. He put me in touch with Maan, and I in turn took photos of her. Shortly after our second shoot, she headed off to Tokyo.

Not much later, my relationship with Arnout ended. Maan sent me a message: "Come to Tokyo!" I impulsively booked a ticket. I'd never flown further than Sweden and now I suddenly found myself on a flight to Japan. For a minute, I panicked: "Am I really going to the other side of the world, to visit someone I've only met twice?" Well I did, and it was amazing. My love for Tokyo was born.

I moved to Amsterdam to be closer to the photography scene, met the agent that would manage my career in the following years, and things were going smoothly. I shot clothing brands, cosmetic companies and magazines like CosmoGirl. And I had one big dream: shooting in Tokyo.

There were plenty of people who wanted to come along. In the end I went with makeup artist A., stylist I., model Jenna and assistant Maan. The fact that I only use some people's initials will give you a clue as to what happened: it ended in drama. Series didn't turn out right or got rejected, and I was left with a loss. In hindsight it's obvious: we had bitten off more than we could chew.

Seven shoots in seven days. If I had known then what I know now, I would have laughed at hearing such plans. We did it because A. and I. wanted to make money. I wasn't interested in that; I just wanted to shoot in Tokyo. The result would look great in my portfolio, but most importantly, it would be the memory of a lifetime. A kind of Disneyland Paris 2.0. But no, there was money to be made, so I had to do seven shoots.

A few things went wrong. Our model Jenna got an eye infection. There was a miscommunication between the Dutch and the Japanese agencies that represented model Merel, a Dutch girl working in Tokyo. We had trouble booking a certain location. The CosmoGirl photos we had taken the first night, looked extremely slutty and we decided unanimously we wanted to do them over. And stylist I. turned out to be a xenophobic bitch.

She complained all day long, and because she shared a room with makeup artist A., she, too, became infected with the negativity. Both ladies got it into their heads that there might be some problems up ahead, and they decided beforehand that they would blame me.

One night they approached me. CosmoGirl had already sent me a few messages, asking how the shoot was coming along. I wanted to tell them honestly ("Sorry, we've had some setbacks, we didn't like the way the first photos turned out, but we're going to do a reshoot tonight!"), but A. and I. told me not to. They were older and more experienced in this industry, so I felt forced to listen to them.

The reshoot went well. The photos were great, even though it was an exhausting evening. "Don't tell any of that to CosmoGirl", the duo said. "Just turn in the photos and act like nothing happened!" It wasn't my MO at all, but I had no choice.

We came home, I turned in the photos and – surprise! – CosmoGirl called: "Bianca, what's this I'm hearing?!"

I felt the colour drain from my face. A. and I. had used

my silence to tell their biased version of the story, in which everything was my fault – from the slutty styling and make-up to the lack of communication. I tried to defend myself but was all too aware that "Yeah but they said…" sounded like pointing fingers, like an irresponsible girl who doesn't own up to her actions. I got screwed. Screwed hard. I didn't care that I lost money; what hurt me was being tossed out of CosmoGirl, the magazine I had loved working for.

But the worst part for me was the fact that they had ruined my Tokyo dream. And so I flew back a few months later, even if it was only for four days. I had to make things right with my favourite place on earth.

The failed photography trip forced me to face facts: I had no idea who to trust or who to listen to anymore. I had allowed myself to fall victim to the duplicity and the fakeness of the fashion world, and although deep down I knew things weren't right, I wasn't able to stand up for myself. All my life people had made me feel so insecure about my communication skills that I was an easy pushover for the sneaky duo.

When people hear about autism and communication problems, they usually think of big things: taking statements like "I waited for a hundred years" literally, or showing downright inappropriate behaviour. In reality it's more like the story above.

Besides the blow I was dealt by the Tokyo trip, the huge pressure to perform and all the last-minute changes were starting to take their toll. The better my career was going, the more prestigious the jobs got, the less I enjoyed it. I was terrified and lived in a constant state of stress. I got so mad at my agent when she'd once again promise a client it would be no problem for me to deliver the edited images the next day. On the other hand I felt I should be grateful to her: she was the one who gave me work, an income.

During that same period, I met the guy I call Mark in this book. "I'm not very good with social stuff and surprises", I told him on one of our first dates. I didn't know yet that I was autistic, but that much I knew about myself. "I don't think it's that bad", Mark said. I would regularly let him talk me into coming along to parties or friends. It's nice when someone believes in you, but at the same time it's devastating when you constantly feel like you're coming up short.

Nearly all social situations were a disaster. Looking back on it now, I know that that had a lot to do with Mark's expectations of me. To his idea of what was "normal". A family visit could easily lead to a big argument afterwards because my way of reacting was not done according to his family.

"You're a photographer!" Mark's father once exclaimed enthusiastically. "Would you like to see the photos I took at Mark's sister's registered partnership ceremony?" I pictured having to feign interest for an entire photo album and having to say "Oh, yes, very nice!" at every photo, because I realised no one was interested in my honest opinion as a professional photographer. I answered, "No, that's alright, thanks", as if politely turning down a second cup of tea. Mark thought I was rude and indifferent. I knew there was no way I could have done it right.

It was a dark period. We were having trouble in our relationship, my work no longer made me happy, and I spent most of my time lying in bed or on the couch. Every time Mark threatened to break up with me, or actually broke up with me, I panicked. I vented by writing all my problems on my blog, to which an acquaintance responded, "Hey, could it be that you have autism?"

The acquaintance in question was autistic herself, and she recognised certain things. She sent me some articles, which I read carefully. Autism. Yes, could be. I remember people saying things like that about my ex Arnout, and how much that angered me at the time. "What do you mean autistic?! You just don't *get* this guy!" Now it started to dawn on me that the reason that I understood Arnout so well, might have been because I was wired the same way. I decided to get tested.

Chapter 4

The diagnosis

Out of a cereal box

The friend who pointed out I may have autism was undergoing therapy herself at a local Autism Centre in North-Holland, and I was able to go there as well. My diagnostic process report, which now has a place in the 'things to keep' folder here at home, starts with my reason for applying.

> *"Client has been referred by her GP at her own request. She wonders if she may have an autism spectrum disorder, more specifically: Asperger Syndrome. There appears to be a lifelong pattern of social ineptitude."*

And then – just like that! – I got my diagnosis, like picking out the prize in a cereal box.

No, it was nothing like that, of course. Although I see plenty of people complaining on social media about how "everybody gets a label nowadays", I can guarantee you it's easier to walk from one end of Scotland to the other without encountering rain.

This diagnostic process involved conversations with me, as well as with people close to me, such as my partner at the time, Mark, and my mother. I filled out several questionnaires and did various tests, partly to rule out other things such as ADD. This is what the report says:

> *"Client doesn't meet the criteria for ADD. Client does appear to have a lot of trouble filtering information. It seems as if nothing gets past her, rather than things*

*escaping her. According to her mother, the client some-
times lives in her own world. She thinks this is a defence
mechanism for the client, to avoid being overwhelmed
by things. The hectic behaviour and impulsiveness, as
described by the client, seem to stem from tension and
clumsiness, from not knowing how to say something
the right way."*

The process took several months. The final report consist-
ed of six pages, assessing item by item to what extent I met
the criteria. It discussed my childhood and also looked at my
current living situation, to make sure my problems weren't of
a temporary nature or caused by external factors. Because
the DSM-5 didn't exist yet (for people without a photograph-
ic memory, you'll find the explanation on page 18), I got my
diagnosis according to the DSM-IV: Asperger Syndrome.

The questionable history of Dr Asperger

Pediatrician Hans Asperger, after whose observations Asperger's Syndrome was named, worked in Vienna under the Nazi regime. As we now know, people with physical or mental disabilities were murdered – or at least sterilised – by the Nazis in huge numbers, in order to create a "perfect" Aryan race. According to researcher Herwig Czech, Asperger contributed to this with his method of diagnosis.[10]

Both Hans Asperger and Simon Baron-Cohen speak of an 'extremely masculine brain' when describing autism. Hans Asperger was even convinced the disorder only occurred in boys. But the book *Asperger's Children*, in which Edith Sheffer – just like Herwig Czech – delves into the history of Dr Asperger in Nazi times, shows that he assessed boys and girls differently.

For example, in the case of Elfriede and Margarete, two thirteen-year-old girls he was treating, he attributed their socially unacceptable behaviour to their menstruation. The fact that one of the girls wasn't even menstruating yet didn't bother him at all. The girls' social ineptitude was the biggest problem; after all, women needed to find a husband, get married and have children. Their academic

10 Czech, Hedwig, 'Hans Asperger, National Socialism, and "race hygiene" in Nazi-era Vienna', Molecular Autism 9, 29 (2018). DOI: 10.1186/s13229-018-0208-6

performances were barely discussed, as opposed to those of boys.

Two boys who were being treated by Asperger, Fritz and Harro, turned out to be just as socially maladjusted. Fritz, for example, had been sent home from kindergarten after a few days because he had attacked other kids. Just like the girls, Fritz and Harro were insolent and didn't do as they were told. Both the boys and the girls showed poor judgement, preferred to be alone and had a "blank, distant look" on their faces. The two boys, however, who also happened to be from richer (but eccentric) families, were the only ones to be diagnosed with "autistic psychopathy". Their violent outbursts were attributed to the disorder because, according to Dr Asperger, autistics just happened to be sadistic and enjoyed their malicious behaviour. The people around them were advised to treat the boys with respect and to give them space to do things their own way. As a result, the boys started functioning a lot better and were able to return to school. The girls, however, did not get diagnosed with autism; they were labelled as having "severe developmental issues" and transferred to Am Spiegelgrund, an institution where a lot of patients were euthanised or died as a result of the facility's abysmal health conditions.

Some researchers say Hans Asperger saved autistic boys – the so-called high-functioning ones – by arguing that their little autistic brains would possibly make them amazing codebreakers for the German army. That might sound great at first, but are autistics only worth something when they're useful to you?

Anna de Hooge is autistic and wrote her thesis on "Aspie supremacy". Her work, entitled *Binary Boys, Autism, Aspie Supremacy and post-Humanist Normativity*, examines prejudices concerning autism and Asperger's Syndrome, in combination with traits such as sex and skin colour.[11] In her work, De Hooge also refers to the aforementioned study by Czech.

In her thesis, De Hooge argues that, although Nazi practices are thankfully a thing of the past, Asperger's harmful sub-division still exists. For example, people speak of "high-functioning" and "low-functioning" autistics, or Asperger's versus classic autism. According to this view, besides social quirks, the label 'Asperger's' – as opposed to classic autism – also comes with special talents, which make the autistic person "useful". Such a sub-division is short-sighted, very black-and-white and, in many cases, harmful.

Furthermore, a lot of people still assume autism is something that mainly affects men, something De Hooge also discusses in her thesis. Right now, autism is diagnosed in men four times as often as in women. This difference used to be even bigger. I was always told this is because women are better at camouflaging and I believed it, until I read Anna's thesis. Are women better at camouflaging, or do they face more severe consequences if they don't?

---

11 Hooge, Anna N. de, 'Binary Boys: Autism, Aspie Supremacy and Post/Humanist Normativity', Disability Studies Quarterly, 39:1, 2019. DOI: 10.18061/dsq.v39i1.6461

My diagnostic report states that "client can only refer to a feeling when she has experienced a similar situation." This is presented as "proof" for my flawed Theory of Mind, and I believed it. It also says, "Client tends to await other people's reactions, so she knows how to respond". I know now that I don't wait because I don't know how to react, but because I know others won't appreciate my response. A survival mechanism developed by a lot of autistic women because "shyness" is still more accepted in women than directness.

Although we've come a long way since the days of Dr Asperger, society still expects different things from women than from men. Women are supposed to be sweet and soft-spoken. When they're angry, people are quick to label them irrational and hysterical, or even hormonal. When they take charge, they're bossy. (To quote the great philosopher Beyoncé: "I'm not bossy. I'm the boss!")

Autistic behaviour in men is better accepted, or swept under the rug with a dismissive "ah well, men…" This can also be seen in TV shows, Anna de Hooge argues in her thesis. She watched shows like *Sherlock* and *The Big Bang Theory* and concluded that the "autistic" characters get away with exceptionally dickish, aggressive or inappropriate behaviour, such as spying on the girl next door or completely ignoring someone else's authority.

Because the image of autism in the media is mainly that of the white male with Asperger's, this is the one most easily recognised. This leads to a certain self-fulfilling prophecy in finding and getting the correct diagnosis and can lead to unpleasant and even dangerous situations for people that don't fit this image, for example when police officers don't recognise a person's peculiar behaviour as autistic.

Women and people of colour are underrepresented in the diagnosed autism population, but as soon as autism occurs simultaneously with intellectual disability, the numbers are a lot closer. Is the white, male, super-smart computer nerd – i.e. the stereotypical man with Asperger's – really more prevalent? Or is there something else going on here? It seems that women and people of colour feel forced to mask their autistic traits, due to a lack of diagnosis and out of fear for the consequences of being different. To what extent they succeed depends on the mental ability of the autistic in question. But it's exhausting, no matter what.

After the diagnosis

Alright, there I was with my autism diagnosis. All of a sudden I knew what was up with me, what kind of books I could start ordering and what I had to work on. I was convinced everything was going to be better, that my relationship with Mark was saved and that I was going to hack my autism. Only the good bits, please. The sensory overload? I was going to learn how to cope with it – in fact, I was just going to let it affect me less and less. Oh, how naive I was.

My relationship with Mark wasn't saved. He read the books I ordered and it only frightened him: "This all sounds really bad, and it's never going to go away!" He saw his future crumble before him. We did try for a while, with the help of coaching and psychoeducation and even Risperdal, an antipsychotic that's also supposed to help people with autism, but to no avail.

It wasn't until after the relationship ended that I *really* started to learn things. I quit taking Risperdal, because although it calmed me down (for once I didn't explode when Mark touched my freshly painted windowsill, for example), I also lost all my creativity and sense of humour. When Mark and I were still together, I thought I needed the medication to be more easy-going. But only after he was out of my life, did I realise it was okay to be myself. My real self, with its positive and negative aspects. I finally realised I needed to accept my autism, along with its limitations and boundaries. I wasn't going to be fun at family outings, no matter how much I'd practice. I wasn't going to be sociable after a hard day's work. Although it felt like a huge loss at first, it turned out to be a liberation in the end.

I do still struggle regularly. In the twenty-five years I didn't know I was autistic, I formed opinions and ideas about everything. They're not at all always right, but they sure are persistent. Expectations, the way I pictured the future... I had to adjust all of them. I'm still learning every day not to be so hard on myself. Which may be even harder when you *know* you're autistic and see so clearly how your behaviour differs from the norm. Sometimes I look at myself as if my soul has left my body and is floating somewhere above. I see myself walking, shoulders up to my ears; I hear myself going on about Disney and Japan. I keep an eye out for every abnormality so I can quickly correct myself as much as I can. Yet I try to be kind, and to rewrite my own story mentally. I'm not a loser. I'm a girl with an invisible handicap.

Daniëlle's story: a late diagnosis

Daniëlle (31) is a fashion-loving girl with coloured hair, a slick blog and two Instagram accounts. At @dutchgirlsinmuseums we see her, together with her partner in crime, pose in spectacular rooms and in front of the most amazing pieces of art Dutch museums have to offer. This social media marketeer knows exactly how to present herself and her ideas to the market. On her profile @allesvandaan.nl she describes herself as an "autism superhero": she got her autism diagnosis eighteen months ago, after several depressions.

Daniëlle: "My first depression actually started when I was about thirteen years old. Now when I read back what I wrote in my diary at the time, it's quite clear — one page says in giant letters: "I hate this, I hate my life!" I also complained about stomach aches a lot. When I was fifteen, I really hit a brick wall. I was exhausted from copying behaviour, from trying to fit in, from acting "normal". I wouldn't go to school for days and eventually had to transfer to a lower-level high school. I had a pretty negative self-image, and I couldn't understand why nothing ever worked out quite right. I was a quiet, shy girl who always stretched herself too thin and gave too much. It felt like a war going on in my head, and it was draining. My parents are still amazed I got my high school diploma, as I never had the energy to study. Luckily I remember everything, so I passed all my exams.

I had always dreamt of doing something in books or magazines, so I knew exactly what I wanted to do after high school: I was going to study Literary Trade & Publishing. But the Amsterdam University of Applied Sciences got with the times and rebranded the stuffy-sounding, bookish programme into the very hip 'Media and Information Management'.

I started at the age of seventeen, among a whole bunch of people who were older and more outspoken than I was. The group assignments were horrible. And the first two exams were nothing like what I had been used to in high school. Everything was so much bigger! I failed the exams, which confirmed my already not-so-positive self-image: "See," I told myself, "you can't do this." I quit my studies after a few months.

The rest of the year I worked several different jobs through a temp agency, with varying levels of success. I started a new course in September: I was going to get my Teaching Certificate for primary school. One of my best friends was going to do the same course. Although studying came easy to me and I enjoyed my internship at a pre-school, I struggled with the interaction with colleagues. I had less and less energy, often called in sick and by March, my journey into Teacher Training had come to an end as well.

Again, I set off to find a job. I found work at a toyshop in my neighbourhood, and even though some people might think a busy environment like that wouldn't work for autistics at all, I flourished. The work was straightforward, structured. I knew exactly what to do, and the counter at the cash register ensured that there was just enough distance between myself and the customers. When it was quiet – which it often was – I had plenty of time to recuperate, tidy up the shop and straighten the shelves. Oh, those wonderful, perfectly neat shelves – I just loved them!

Meanwhile I thought about my future, and came to the conclusion I still wanted to do something in books and magazines. I enrolled in the Media and Information Management programme for a second time. Because I was able to explain my first, failed attempt with an official depression diagnosis, I was allowed to start again with a clean slate.

Things went much better this time. I was a few years older and I already knew what to expect. It was still intense, though. When I came home, I'd immediately lock myself in my room with the lights turned off and my laptop on. Destimulation is what I would call it looking back. "We thought you didn't like our company!" my parents told me recently.

During my studies, I did several internships. That went well, as long as I had a mentor who understood me. My work was always fine, but I was still a quiet girl who was often sick from sensory overload. If I didn't get along well with my internship mentor, I would usually blame myself. But all in all, I still managed. My job at the Amsterdam Public Library was perfect. I felt right at home there surrounded by books, I knew what to do and arranging the books made me super happy! And whenever people asked me something I didn't know the answer to, I had a little trick up my sleeve: I would show them how to look up things in our computer system themselves.

After I had finished my studies, I got a job at a media agency that did marketing and social media for large companies. That hectic environment actually didn't suit me at all. My work was fine, all my co-workers told me, but I didn't join in any after-work drinks or nights out. I was too quiet, too weird... There was just no connection. I tried to copy behaviour, to adjust, but because I couldn't completely deny who I was I'd compensate by wearing that striking vintage dress, while they all went around wearing the same T-shirt. After three six-month contracts it was done: I wasn't getting a permanent contract. Not entirely unexpected.

As I was also moving house and going through a renovation during this period, plus I was reducing the amount of antidepressants I had been taking for years, I had a total breakdown. I got so depressed all I wanted to do was die. But I'd promised my mother not to commit suicide, and I don't like to break a promise. I went to the Mental Health Emergency Service and was sent to the outpatient clinic at the hospital, where I met the best psychologist ever. "Have you ever considered getting tested for autism?" she asked.

I started laughing. I'd been telling myself to "stop being so autistic" for years, but it had never occurred to me that I might actually *be* autistic. My boyfriend Oscar thought it was a ridiculous notion at first: "They're trying to talk you into things!". My mother didn't believe it either. They all had this Rain Man image in their heads, and frankly, so did I."

There's so very much I recognise in Daniëlle's story. I, too, often don't fit in with the rest of the group because I skip after-work drinks and nights out. I, too, wear unusual outfits to still feel a bit like myself. I, too, used to think all autistics were like Rain Man. But Daniëlle isn't like Rain Man, she's like me. We both got diagnosed late because we were forced to learn to camouflage. It was our way of surviving, but it wasn't sustainable and eventually took its toll.

Sander's story: looking for help

Even if you're the quintessential white, male computer nerd, lots of people still won't be able to recognise your autism, let alone offer adequate help. Sander (39) had a breakdown in 2012, and it took him two and a half years to get a correct diagnosis. But that didn't mean he was home free just yet.

Sander: "My downward spiral actually really started in 2007, when my father died. He was a lot like me and had always been able to give me good advice. When I lost him, it felt as if my whole safety net had suddenly disappeared. I had always been self-employed, but now the opportunity arose to get a job at a small chain store, I grabbed that opportunity with both hands. My girlfriend at the time was without a job, so I thought: security, that's what we need!

Soon enough, I realised some things weren't quite right at work. Bonuses and pay rises that had been promised to me kept falling through at the last minute, my job description didn't match what I was actually doing and I was forced to work harder and harder and do more overtime without getting paid.

If he'd still been alive, my father probably would have urged me to leave. But I stayed. I told myself I was worthless: I had – probably due to my then-undiagnosed autism – no diplomas. My current role didn't technically exist and all the IT work I had done for the company up until then was for internal use, so I wouldn't have anything to show for it. I told myself I was going to wait until the webshop I had built from scratch was launched. At least then I would have something to prove my skills.

I continued on with the last bit of energy I had left. I kept powering through, until I simply couldn't go on anymore. I had to stop. I didn't take sick leave; I was too proud for that. I resigned with my head held high. Very foolish, in hindsight.

I started my own IT company and soon found several great clients. But I was so drained from my previous job, that things soon started going downhill after the initial start-up rush. I stayed in bed for days at a time. I thought I had a burn-out. But no matter what I tried – conversations with psychologists, mindfulness, yoga, sports, medication – I just couldn't get my energy levels back up. It took more than a year before anyone thought of autism. And another year on a waiting list before I was finally diagnosed.

My relationship, which had already suffered a lot during my last job, didn't survive. I moved back to Groningen, a change that had a big impact in itself. The psychiatrist I ended up with was far too optimistic about my situation and gradually started reducing my antidepressants. This resulted in a huge relapse.

All this time, I had managed to keep my head above water using my savings, the little bit of work I could handle and some help from my mother, among other people. But now I really hit rock bottom financially, and it was time to ask for help. I dragged myself over twenty imaginary shame thresholds and went to social services.

I thought I came pretty well prepared. It was clear what

had caused my situation, I had made specific plans with a client to get back on top of things, my intention to use as little "free money" as possible was evident from everything I had done up to this point in my life – as well as from the fact that I had waited until the very, very last moment to ask for help. I had found information about the 'BBZ', a financial aid plan for independent contractors who have hit a rough patch. Exactly what I needed.

The civil servant didn't think so. He merely glanced at my figures and plans, completely ignored my autism diagnosis and depression and asked why I was "only now" asking for help. The fact that I'd tried to make it on my own for as long as I could now completely backfired on me. The civil servant called my company "hopeless" and "a hobby", something he wasn't prepared to pay for. I wanted to make all sorts of objections, but I was beat. Stunned and numb, without any hope of a solution, I returned home."

Social services decided that running his own business wouldn't suit Sander, despite the fact that being independent would give him the flexibility to deal with sensory overload. The Social Support Act official he spoke to next treated him like a little kid and didn't consider him capable of managing his personal state-provided budget. She suggested jobs like loading dishwashers or sorting nuts and bolts. All this time Sander was perfectly clear: *this* is what I can do, *this* is what I want, *this* is what I need from you guys. Nobody listened.

I see this a lot: several autistics I know with unmistakable talents were told not to start their own company because it "wouldn't suit autistics". Those who wanted to start one anyway risked losing all safety nets. And this, while there are plenty of autistics who *did* get the chance and are now flourishing in their field. A good example is Laura Brouwers, who is professionally known as Cyarin and who is world famous for her illustrations.

Luckily things turned out alright in the end for Sander, when he eventually came across a wonderful care-providing institution that looked after him. This organisation arranged for Sander to retroactively get his social benefits and helped him almost immediately, despite the fact that it took ten (!) months for his support to come through via the Social Support Act.

Ups and downs

Even specialised care, where you'd expect people to know more about autism, often leaves a lot to be desired. Waiting lists are long, and if you're doing alright for just a little bit too long, you lose all support. For instance, roughly a year and a half ago, I asked for help at my local GGZ, a mental health care institution where I'd done a programme before. A media company had contacted me for a large project which would start four months later, and because I knew it was going to be tough, I decided to ask for help. With plenty of time still, or so I thought. Alas: it had been just over a year since I'd last been there, so they had closed my file and I had to start all over again. Which meant a three-month waiting list and a new diagnostic process. This all seemed quite unnecessary to me – autism doesn't go away, after all. They mumbled something about health insurance.

I resigned myself to the situation and trusted that at least I had applied early enough to get help in time. The diagnostic process showed that I – shocker – was still autistic. I was assigned a case handler, met with her and explained my situation. And then she quit her job.

The replacing case handler couldn't see me until six weeks later. This man didn't know me nor my story, plus we wouldn't even be able to actually start working together until I was already three quarters into my tough project. I got angry and told the institution this wouldn't help me at all. That was fine with them, but they still went ahead and claimed a thousand euros on my health insurance. I went through a difficult time with lots of panic attacks and only help from friends and family to see me through. It turned out alright in the end, but no thanks to the GGZ.

The problem is that institutions often fail to look at the lives of autistic people as a whole, something that was addressed by Jasper Wagteveld, fellow autistic and ambassador of the Dutch Autism Society, at the Society's fortieth anniversary. Ups and downs are inevitable, but what we're seeing is that help is discontinued when someone is going through an 'up' period. "You're doing great!" says the institution, upon which they happily close the file and cash in the insurance money. Then when a 'down' period follows, it takes a long time to start up the process again. A person will have to tell their story for the umpteenth time, get on a waiting list or go through a diagnostic process. This must improve.

According to Jasper, there should be a network where autistic people can go to for help at any point in their lives. If they require some extra care for a while, the intensity is increased. If things are going well, care can be scaled back. But care is always within reach.

I wholeheartedly agree with Jasper. Plus, I think it would work out better for the insurance companies and government institutions that dictate this policy too. A person who receives care sooner won't go downhill as much and will therefore cost less. It's sad that this is how we must look at it, but I'm afraid it's the way things are nowadays.

Chapter 5

Boundaries and limitations

How do you prevent an autistic from ending up at home with a burn-out, a depression, an eating disorder or other self-harming behaviour? The key is to know and respect your boundaries and limitations. In the following part, I'll discuss listening to your body, designing your own life, and the blessings and horrors of coaching.

Originally, in the first draft of this book, this chapter was titled 'Interview with Melissa in New York'. Yes, I was supposed to go to New York to visit Melissa, a model who I've known for a long time – I was the one who scouted her years ago at the ElleGirl forum. I was going to bring Riemer along, get the gang together. But I'm not in New York, I'm in The Hague. Next week, I'm flying out to Tokyo for the second time during this writing process and the second time this year. Uh-oh, is that me deviating from my plan just like that?! Yep, it is, and I have three reasons to do so:

1. Melissa's life in New York is very unpredictable
2. I was anxious and suffering from bad stomach aches at the time I decided this
3. Tokyo just suits me better

In short: I came up against my limitations, and I listened.

Melissa's story: Concrete jungle where dreams are made of

Melissa Koole (25) is a model. A curvy model. A top model. Even if you've never heard of her, you've probably seen her plenty of times. Melissa is one of those models who may not have the fame, but she does have the job. She poses for big labels such as Mango and Vera Wang, regularly flies from New York via Spain to Germany and back in one week and – let's not beat around the bush – rakes in the big bucks. She's the main breadwinner in her relationship, and her husband got a US visa as *her* spouse. Oh, and she's autistic.

Melissa: "I was an unusual but happy child. I was more interested in nature than in other kids and I knew everything there was to know about birds and insects. I was horrified by anything sticking to my skin, which was a disaster in combination with my sun allergy. When I had trouble speaking as a child, I started seeing a speech therapist who suggested I should be tested for autism. My parents, very down-to-earth farmers from the Dutch Westland, didn't think that was necessary; I might have behaved differently, but I wasn't crazy!

Yet all through elementary school, I felt like the weird one, and I was fed up with it. So when I started high school, I decided I was going to fit in. I told my mother: "From now on, I'm only going to wear jeans." I swapped my usual comforta-ble outfit for ones that caused a sensory overload – but hey, they were hip and cool – and started drinking and hanging out with older teenagers when I was thirteen. I didn't realise my longing to be "normal" was putting me in danger.

One of the older boys forced me to perform certain sexual acts on him. I didn't want to and I'd told him so, but I still blamed myself. Had I been clear enough? Had I been sending him the wrong signals? The boy told the whole school how "easy" I was and I got horribly bullied for that for the rest of my high school years.

I got depressed and resorted to obsessive behaviour. First I put all my energy into my dream of becoming a model, for which I had to lose some centimeters. Instead of simply working out and eating healthy, "the measurements" took over my whole life. When I finally realised – after several years – that I was destroying myself, I stopped modelling and went on to study Business Administration.

Although I had no trouble studying, I had underestimated the impact of this sudden change. I often found myself on the bus to university without a clue what I was doing. I would sometimes self-harm by pulling out my hair. In my second year at university, I finally took the step to see my GP and seek help. When I was nineteen, I received my diagnosis: autism.

My boyfriend (now husband) Joost is the one who helped me get through it all. He isn't autistic, but he understands me very well. The diagnosis itself helped as well, I finally had an explanation, and I knew there were more people like me."

Pushing boundaries

Most undiagnosed autistics keep pushing – and crossing – their own boundaries. They make choices they don't really want to make, because others tell them it's fun or that's just the way they should behave. When an autistic person says that something is too loud or too bright, the answer usually is: "Get over it!" We are taught to ignore signals, to suck it up, and to definitely not listen to ourselves. People who have recently been diagnosed with autism often don't even know their own boundaries anymore; the uncomfortable feeling is so omnipresent, that listening to it seems like an impossible task.

Melissa's life now seems to have taken an 180-degree turn. After her graduation, she decided to give modelling another shot, this time without having to lose weight: she became a curvy model. She signed a contract in New York and soon after, her career took flight. As is usually the case in the unpredictable world of modelling, she often doesn't know until the last minute when she'll have time off, or where on earth she'll – literally – be working the following week. Her base is New York, a city I personally found extremely overstimulating during my one and only visit there. So my question to Melissa is: how do you manage that?!

Melissa: "The first time I went to New York for a modelling job, it was very intense for me as well. I stayed inside all the time. And I didn't eat properly, because I didn't know what to expect and where to go. At a certain point I said to myself:

if things stay like this, I'm going to quit. Then I'm just not cut out for this work.

Yet, four years later, I'm still at it. What helps, is that I didn't move to New York immediately; I commuted for about two and a half years. That way I got to know the city, the noises, the shops. Now Joost and I live in Brooklyn, in a neighbourhood with low-rise buildings and a lot of European influences. I could never live in Manhattan, way too busy.

My work is unpredictable, but within that, I try to create as much predictability as possible. For example, I've agreed with my agency that they'll provide me with as many details as possible, as early as possible. Thanks to that I know before most other models when and where I'll be travelling, on which airline, and which hotel I'll be staying in.

I learnt through trial and error: when I just started out, there were times I needed to find dinner for myself in a strange city while I was already completely overstimulated. If the restaurant I picked turned out to be full or closed, I didn't know what to do. But going to bed without having dinner is asking for trouble the next day, so I now keep lists in Google Maps of all the restaurants I've been to before. If I'm not familiar with a city yet, I'll ask colleagues for tips. In the taxi on my way to the airport I'll take the time to look up ten other restaurants, to have alternatives.

Although my agency does a good job keeping me up to speed, there's always a possibility they'll call to say I have to be ready to fly off to Timbuktu in three hours. That's why I always keep a packed suitcase in my closet. Depending on the weather I'll add some extra clothes, but then I'm ready to go.

By now I know almost all airlines and where to find the good seats. I know my way around most airports and I have special earplugs that filter out most background noise. I also have more and more regular clients, who return every month or season. That creates predictability, not just in my schedule, but also in my workday: I know the team, know if I can expect a nice lunch and have a fair idea of the number of outfits we'll be shooting.

And of course my husband Joost is my rock. It was hard at times when I'd already moved to New York and he was still living in the Netherlands. I like to talk about what's bothering me in order to clear my head, but I also benefit immensely from the deep touch pressure technique. Think of it as a really firm hug that calms you down. It's a nice technique for Joost as well; this way he can physically do something to help me. Plus, a hug is always good for your relationship, right?

During shoots, I generally don't talk about my autism, unless I've been booked specifically for my "story". When I'm working, I usually put on an imaginary mask. After all, American clients do tend to expect a bubbly, high-energy personality. It's become sort of a strategy for me that I know will bring in a lot of business.

It's logical that I put up a mask around clients, but sometimes I feel like I can't quite be myself even around friends and people I know. People often tell me, "Melissa, you're doing so well, we can't even tell anything's the matter with you!" They mean well, but it does make me feel like there's no room to really be myself when I'm not doing so well. I think it's even trickier for women than it is for men: it's less acceptable for us to be angry or closed off, let alone have a foot-stomping, screaming meltdown.

At home I try to compensate for all the stimuli my work fires at me. I usually eat the same thing and tend not to try anything new. I go to the supermarket I'm familiar with, work out in the same place I always work out. When I have a day off, I enjoy doing nothing. I curl up on the couch under a blanket and watch Netflix, do logic puzzles such as sudoku, or delve into the world of birds. Seeing a rare species of bird can make me really happy."

Plans versus options

As an autistic, I've learnt one thing from my coaches: to plan. I mean, I've learnt more than that of course, but planning was supposed to be the Holy Grail; the ultimate key to preventing overstimulation, the ultimate way to add structure and order to my life, and therefore the ultimate solution to guarding my own boundaries. Yet at times, my planning was only moderately successful. And then one of my friends said something that made me think:

"I don't have plans, I have options."

Hermione ("What do you want your pseudonym to be in my book?" – "Hermione sounds good!" – "Sure hon, no problem.") is not autistic, but she has a child. She quickly learnt that you can make a hundred plans, but they all go straight in the bin the minute your little angel wakes up vomiting.

I don't have a child, but I do recognise the issue. Sometimes I'm the one who wakes up feeling completely overstimulated. I can predict this to a certain extent, but those predictions aren't infallible. Planning therefore used to be largely guesswork: how tired will this make me, and how much time will I need to recover? If I failed to plan enough time to recuperate, I'd get overstimulated and would have to redo my whole planning. Stress! If I'd scheduled in too much time, I would suddenly find myself at home with an empty day ahead and no idea what to do, usually having finished everything on my to-do list by then – reluctantly and under pressure.

Simply put, the planning system was far from ideal. And that's when Hermione came along with her 'options'. A whole list of things she *could* do. She didn't have to, but she could. And honestly, a lot of my activities could easily go on the 'options' list as well. Editing photos, writing a blog post... Unless I have a client with a strict deadline, it really doesn't matter *if* and *when* exactly I do things. Melissa told me something similar about the weeks in which business is quiet: "I have a list in my phone of things I could do one day, like buying a new pot for one of our plants."

You might worry that with a loose planning like that, you'll end up getting nothing done at all. But that's not the case. Once I'd started on my website, I became so enthusiastic I wanted to keep working on it every day. And this method has another advantage: the things that *really* make you happy will reveal themselves almost organically.

Naoki Higashida, an autistic Japanese boy who hardly speaks, also explains in his book *The reason I jump* how he believes visual day planners, which are often used for autistic children, aren't ideal.

"*I understand any plan is only a plan, and is never definite, but I just cannot take it when a fixed arrangement does not proceed as per the visual schedule. I understand that changes can't always be avoided, but my brain shouts back: No way, that's not acceptable. So speaking for myself, I'm not a big fan of having visual schedules around the place. People with autism may look happier with pictures and diagrams of where we're supposed to be and when, but in fact we end up being restricted by them. They make us feel like robots, with each and every action pre-programmed. What I'd suggest is that instead of showing us visual sched-ules, you talk through the day's plan with us, verbally and beforehand. Visual schedules create such a strong impression on us that if a change occurs, we get flus-tered and panicky."*[12]

The interview with Melissa *was* in my day planner, it was on paper. It wasn't an option, it was a plan. Still, I decided not to go, and do the interview in a different way. I didn't want to run the risk of ending up in New York while Melissa just hap-pened to be working in Spain that week. I also didn't want to run the risk of becoming completely overstimulated in that busy city, which would cause the rest of my work to take a huge blow. And then there was that other doom scenario: stomach aches.

---

12 Higashida, Naoki. *'The reason I jump'* Translated by K.A. Yoshida and David Mitchell, 2013

Stomach aches

Sometimes it seems as if autistics are allergic to everything, or at least have stronger reactions to lots of things. As a child, I wasn't allowed to have any food colourants – not because they made me overactive, but because I'd nearly choke on my own saliva. Nearly every artificial substance gives me a rash, medication tends to have weird side effects on me, and stomach aches are the thing from which I've been suffering most over the past few years.

I get cramps, acute diarrhoea and really just have to stay indoors the rest of the day. If I stay inside, generally, nothing else happens. If I force myself to go out though, the cramps hit me with a vengeance, usually right at the moment my toiletless train suddenly stops at a red sign. "It's all in your head!" I used to scold myself. "No, it's lactose intolerance!" the figure on my other shoulder would say. I avoided lactose, and that seemed to help. I swapped milk for soy milk, ice cream for vegan ice cream. But after a while, I developed an oversensitivity to soy! And even now, having traded soy milk for almond milk, my stomach still manages to ruin my day sometimes.

There are theories stating that autism stems from unhealthy gut flora. Supporters of these theories usually base this on studies in which the intestinal bacteria of autistic people with intestinal problems were exchanged for a healthier mix, after which the autistics' behaviour improved. But before you put yourself or your child on some kind of extreme diet: all this research has shown is that people without stomach aches tend to be more pleasant. How pleasant are you when you're sick? Exactly, just as I thought.

The reality is that it's still not clear what the connection is. Are intestinal problems the cause of autism? Or an effect? There's a lot to be said for the latter, because constantly having stress hormones run rampant through your body isn't all too great for your gut flora either. We all know the expression: "He nearly shat his pants" when referring to someone who's scared. Perhaps both autism and intestinal problems are the result of an anomaly in a specific gene or a specific part of the brain – that's another possibility. Or maybe we don't just have a stronger reaction to sensory stimuli, but also to stimuli coming from inside our intestines, or stimuli given off by certain foods.

All I know for sure so far, is that my intestinal problems are worse when the rest of me is overstimulated as well. "Maybe that's something you should be thankful for", a New Age hippie-type once told me. "Maybe the stomach cramps are your body telling you you've reached your limit." Although I felt myself getting agitated, I'm afraid she was right. I used to get headaches, but I ignored them until I started getting panic attacks. And even those I tried to suppress with medication or breathing exercises. These stomach aches, though, are one thing I'm afraid to ignore. It's a limitation I *have* to respect. It's a shame that, at times, I reach this limit much sooner than I'd like to, but maybe it's something I should indeed be thankful for: I don't want to know what would happen if I lived *without* restrictions.

Tokyo suits me better

Apart from the stomach ache-slash-overstimulation and Melissa's unpredictable schedule, there was another reason I decided not to go to New York: I could only spend the money I had saved once. And I missed Tokyo.

I talked before about my realisation that social norms are all just 'made up'. New York is so very different from Tokyo. In New York, people stare at you on the subway; in Tokyo, nobody looks at you. In New York, everyone speaks very loud, in Tokyo, the entire Starbucks knows when two Americans walk in. City noise is so much louder in New York than it is in Tokyo, with sirens blaring every couple of minutes, cars honking, and lots of heavy traffic. In Tokyo, electric cars zoom past virtually without a sound. Different cities, countries and cultures have taught me that I can choose to be where I feel most comfortable. I've chosen Tokyo, and that's why I chose to interview Melissa via WhatsApp. Melissa understood where I was coming from: "I'd probably go absolutely mad in Tokyo, but for you, it's where you are at peace. That's what New York is to me."

According to the norm

It's good to know your boundaries and limitations, but it might be even more important to realise that the boundaries, limitations, norms and values of autistic people aren't necessarily the same as those of the majority. A lot of autistics I know have a much freer view of relationships and sexuality. They're open to polyamory, for example, identify as pansexual or asexual, or feel like they don't quite fit into the standard gender roles society dictates. Of course this isn't the case for everyone: there are plenty of autistics who dream of living out the whole white-picket-fence scenario with a monogamous partner of the opposite sex and 1.6 children. But the difference is so remarkable Reubs Walsh, an autistic transgender herself, devoted a study to it.[13]

Walsh and her team's research shows that 15% of participants, autistic people who were approached via the Netherlands Autism Register, describe themselves as nonbinary or transgender. The national percentage is less than 4%. Especially in people born female it's an extraordinary spike: 21.6% say they don't identify with the gender identity that matches their birth sex. Why is that?

Walsh: "The most probable hypothesis is that the higher percentage is caused by a diminished sensitivity to social

13 Walsh, Reubs J., Krabbendam, L., DeWinter, J. en Begeer, S., 'Brief Report: Gender Identity Differences in Autistic Adults: Associations with Perpetual and Socio-cognitive Profiles', *Journal of Autism and Developmental Disorders*, 48: 12, 4070-4078, 2018. DOI: 10.1007/s10803-018-3702-y

pressure. People with autism care less about other people's perceptions and adhering to the norm. I think this is an example of *flattened priors*, a theory by researcher Liz Pellicano. The theory describes how people with autism put less value on "priors", past experiences. They have a better view of what's *really* going on, rather than making assumptions. It's the same characteristic that tends to make autistics good at analytical work, but also the characteristic that overwhelms them because of the abundance of stimuli that are processed as new information every time."

Furthermore, a survey held by the Netherlands Autism Register shows that 27% of the autistics born female and 12% of the autistics born male describe themselves as bisexual, as opposed to 3% of the average Dutch population. This, too, is a case of flattened priors, according to Reubs.

Walsh: "Autistics are able to look at themselves more clearly and are less inclined to adjust to society's norm. So anyone who has at some point experienced same-sex feelings has no problem describing themselves as bisexual, while a neurotypical person might be more inclined to sweep the experience under the rug by saying something like, "Ah, it only happened once!" or "We were young and experimenting!"

So it might not actually be the case that a different gender identity or sexual orientation is more prevalent in people with autism – it just transpires sooner. Do we just care less about what people think of us?

Walsh: "It goes deeper than that. There's also a difference

on a subconscious level. Neurotypical people are less likely to notice something might be going on with them, because subconsciously they've already labeled themselves. Someone like that may *think* they're cisgender and heterosexual, but something might be brewing underneath the surface."

Walsh's study caught my attention because I recognised myself in it: I've personally never felt quite represented by the label 'woman'. I wouldn't want to change myself, but I also won't be forced into meeting certain expectations. I don't want kids, don't wear makeup and generally don't feel targeted when people make jokes about "typical women" – you know, the jealous, gossiping, forever-shopping stereotypes in high heels. It bothered me that the guys in high school teased me for being flat-chested, but I never wanted my breasts to be bigger. Flat is fine.

To be clear: I have no issues with my biological sex, it's fine with me that my passport says Female and I'm also OK with people addressing me with 'she' and 'her', but somewhere deep down, I think: whatever. I'm not a part of this. I'm just happy to live in a time and a country where that's barely an issue.

I feel pretty much the same way when it comes to relationships. I'm attracted to both men and women, am intrigued by polyamory and although I'm in a relationship at the moment, we don't live together. We did use to live together, by the way. "Oh dear, well, I guess things aren't going very well!" Wrong – things are fine.

They were less fine for a while, though. After selling his house a few months earlier, Riemer moved in with me, and we shared my super cool loft house in Zaandam. It was an old factory, well, part of it. The ceilings were about six meters high, ideal for my photo studio-slash-office. It had a mezzanine across the whole length of the house, from which you could see directly into the studio. That's where we lived and slept.

With the exception of the bathroom and toilet, our house had no rooms. And although at first we had a really good time there together, the lack of me-time started to become an issue. Riemer, who brought three guitars and a keyboard when he moved in, never played music anymore. I was often lying on my bed scrolling through my phone, because I felt restricted too. We didn't want to bother each other, and as a result, ended up doing nothing at all. Fortunately for me, Riemer sometimes left to go to work. Although, fortunately... I was surrounded by my work all the time.

I looked forward to my trips to Japan, but I also regularly booked a hotel for myself in the Netherlands. When I had to be somewhere early, but also when I was simply spent. At the same time I felt guilty: living together had been *my* idea; it would be cheaper, and nice. But just when Riemer had sold his house, I decided I needed a place of my own? Great.

We started getting into arguments, I started staying over at friends' more often, and when I came back after living on my own in Japan for three months, I couldn't adjust anymore. At first I tried to break up the relationship, but I realised pretty soon that *that* wasn't what I wanted. Still, thanks to certain patterns that had become ingrained, it seemed like the only solution. Moving apart as a couple, that's not something you do, right?

We did. Riemer found an apartment in a luxury tower block in Rotterdam, something he had dreamt of for years. I opted for a studio. Not a photo studio this time, but a one-room apartment in The Hague. Centrally located, cheap, and completely self-contained, except for the shared washing machine. It was an apartment just like the one I lived in in Japan. I didn't think such things existed in the Netherlands, but I looked, and I found.

It turned out to be the best solution ever. I unwound. Riemer unwound. So now when we see each other, we *really* pay attention to one another. People sometimes ask me when I plan to move. "Nobody would want to live on twenty-four square meters", they seem to think. But why not? I have less stuff, less stimuli, lower costs... I can spend a month in Japan without having to put my apartment on Airbnb (and thereby running the risk of finding the place ruined when I come home) and things like cleaning and tidying up take me two hours tops. I wouldn't want it any other way.

About coaching

Coaching is one of the instruments that is often used to help autistics shape their lives and learn how to deal with their boundaries and limitations. Unlike seeing a psychologist, coaching is usually practical in nature. With a coach, you might for example look at your planning, your daily routines, at difficult events that lie ahead and at ways to make those situations more manageable. With the help of my coach, I learnt to recognise and respect my boundaries, got practical tips such as incorporating rest and travel time in my daily planner (because yes, travelling takes energy too, and if you're always sick or tired the day after a shoot, you'd better take that into account) and reaching out for help. Riemer once came along to a coaching session so in the future, he would be able to help me manage my weekly schedule. We now share a calendar in Google Calendar. When a week is starting to fill up, he usually hits the brakes before I do: "Does all this really have to be done now?" Usually there are a few things that can be cancelled.

A failed trip

The nicest coaching experience Riemer and I had was with Barbara, autism coach with real-life experience. After a holiday that didn't go so well – we both kept hitting (and exceeding) our limits but were too tired to address it – we had plenty to discuss.

We were going to go on a weeklong journey across western Japan to visit a famous bridge, a village with hot springs (*onsen*) in which you could boil eggs, a city named Obama, and snow monkeys. But we didn't see Obama or the monkeys. Riemer went back home halfway through our trip, after I broke up with him in a moment of total panic. Holy fuck, what happened there?!

In short: I couldn't handle it anymore. The journey. The constant monitoring if everything was alright, the responsibility, the lack of feedback. Every decision I had to make (and there were a lot, starting with changing the booking of our first hotel because the night train we had planned to take turned out to be full) came with a nagging sense of guilt, an adrenaline-pumping insecurity: "Am I doing the right thing? What does Riemer think of this?"

Riemer was pretty sick when he got off the plane. A combination of catching a cold after a Toto concert, a terrible jet lag and a period of grief and stress, caused by the death of his father. So instead of being able to relax the first two days in Tokyo, Riemer was in bed, sick, in his own single hotel room, while I was trying to change the booking of our hotel in Matsue. Afterwards I fell into a black hole because for once, *I* didn't want to be the one starting off a holiday sick or stressed out over work, and therefore, I hadn't planned a thing.

Three days after Riemer's arrival, we set off from Tokyo on our roundtrip. Riemer still hadn't fully recovered. The journey involved a *Shinkansen* (high-speed train) to Okayama and an exceptionally long, hot, bumpy train ride to Matsue. I navigated us towards our newly booked hotel: two single rooms, a twenty-minute walk from the station. A bit far. A bit of an old hotel, too. But hey, it was affordable and available and turned out to serve an amazing breakfast. Not that Riemer ate any of it, the first day. He was still too nauseous.

We had planned to visit a famous bridge, which had gone viral on social media because of extremely distorted shots that made it look much steeper than it actually was. But of course we didn't know that beforehand. (Tip for everyone: the "rollercoaster bridge" is a hoax. Don't fall for it!)

The bridge was a bit out of the way. I was worried about cramps and toilets, google-mapped my butt off and eventually came up with a plan that required Riemer's help. Things like that, you have to ask him explicitly. It's not clear enough if you mumble something about being scared to take a taxi because that would mean you'd have to communicate with the driver. I'd rather walk, I'd rather take a slow old country train that would take way longer – anything to avoid taking a taxi. But sometimes it's the only option, and "This scares me" is my way of saying: "Dude, handle this for me".

When I was travelling around Hong Kong a few weeks earlier with Maan, we'd had no trouble dividing our tasks. I found out which bus we needed to take and made sure Maan got on that same bus. Maan then organised the boat trip to the island, price negotiations and all. It all happened organically, without having to discuss anything.

Somehow it didn't work that way with Riemer. This holiday went wrong, the last holiday went wrong, and both times I heard myself say: "I want to know what's on your mind!" I want to know what's happening, what he's thinking and feeling. Without this feedback, I become more and more insecure, and my stress levels go through the roof. After four days, I collapsed. I couldn't handle the responsibility anymore.

It was as if I was dragging along a boulder. I kept looking behind me: is Riemer still there? Is he okay? I would subtly fish for confirmation ("Wow, pretty nice view, don't you think?"), or less subtly: "Are you still enjoying yourself?" The answers I got were short: "Huh, what? Yeah, why?" I felt my arms and legs go heavy. Maybe I'm too impatient, I thought to myself. Maybe I should give him time. But every time I did just that, nothing happened. Well, nothing, except that my tension and annoyance levels rose to a point where I had to react, like a mosquito bite that itches and itches until you just have to scratch it. Then I'd take charge again: "Come on, let's get a bite to eat."

The first night in Yumura Onsen, the village with the hot spring, we ended up in an *izakaya* (café) that would horrify a health inspector. The elderly couple who ran the place didn't speak a word of English, the menu was handwritten, which made Google Translate useless, and Kei wasn't answering her messages, so we had to figure it out together. Riemer was smart enough to look at what his neighbour was having and ordered the same. I was able to translate *omuraisu* (omelette with rice) and so I ordered that. This may have been my favourite part of the trip. We were together. We were figuring it out together. And despite the roaring insecurity in the background ("Help, where on earth did I take Riemer this time?!"), it seemed that he saw this as a bit of an adventure as well.

But then came day two. We locked ourselves in our hotel room and slept. We were in an *onsen* town, in a fancy hotel with an in-house hot-spring bath, and we didn't go there. I was afraid to. I was beat. I couldn't handle doing any more new things. Having to explain to Riemer how an *onsen* works and leaving him by himself in the men's bath. "Jesus," you might say, "Riemer's not a baby, is he?!" True. And yet I felt extremely responsible, and at the same time totally annoyed.

I like Riemer when I can see inside his head, when he manages to inspire me, when he knows what he wants, when he has an opinion. When I can switch off that sense of responsibility and insecurity because I know *he's* in charge for a bit. When I know things are okay. The last time I saw him that way was at one of his work parties. Riemer was in his element. He was chatting with his co-workers about the company, we were talking to a co-worker and his girlfriend about Japan and our upcoming trip... Riemer *was* someone, big and strong, and when I couldn't take the sound of the party band anymore, we went home without a fuss.

How very different this holiday felt. I took a bath – in the small bath tub in our hotel room, not in the *onsen*. I felt a panic attack coming on. Headache. I managed to calm myself down in the tub, but decided I needed to talk to Riemer afterwards.

"I want to go back to Tokyo", I said, knowing what I was setting in motion.

Evil voices in my head immediately piped up: "You ruin all holidays!" Yes, there is some truth to that. I'm not great at holidays. Ask Mark. Too autistic. "Uhm, hello," the more reasonable voice said, "don't just blame yourself. There's two of you here." Oh right, Riemer. Just as autistic as I am. If not more. But while I have this super stressful control mechanism that makes me check every five minutes if everything's still okay, he doesn't have that at all. On the one hand a blessing, but on the other hand... Let me put it this way: if you don't automatically pick up on how I'm doing and don't actively check either, and if you only act when you see me cry – that's too late. *Way* too late.

Riemer booked himself onto the next plane back to the Netherlands. Perhaps a bit of an overreaction, because while he was still at his hotel at Narita Airport, we finally started talking to each other, *actually* talking (well – via chat that is). We quickly agreed: we need to get help for this. Because we didn't feel like being on a waiting list for six months, because Riemer wasn't particularly interested in getting a diagnosis, and because we were lucky enough to be able to afford it, we decided to hire a private coach. Her name was Barbara de Leeuw, and I knew her already because I contributed to her book *Overprikkeling voorkomen* ("Preventing Sensory Overload"). Riemer emailed her, and she could see us right away.

The right way

After a first meeting just with Riemer, in which he was asked to specifically formulate the reason for his visit, we made an appointment for the two of us together. Barbara analysed: "I saw two autistic people, a strenuous trip and a sick man. Both parties were completely overwhelmed. In Riemer this resulted in impeded functioning, in Bianca in panic and subsequently a longing for security that Riemer couldn't offer at that time."

Barbara pointed out our assumptions and the holes in our communication. "Nobody can see inside someone else's head. What someone says or shows and what they really feel and experience are often two different things. Many people tend to guess other people's emotions based on their words and behaviour, only to come to an incorrect conclusion. That's exactly what I'm trying to prevent."

Barbara made us reflect on what exactly went wrong and think about possible solutions. We looked back on our failed holiday and came to the conclusion that our travel plans, which may have been too ambitious to begin with, should probably have been cancelled – or at least adjusted – back in Tokyo. Even though it had been planned, even though it was a waste of a train ticket, even though we had been looking forward to it – someone should have said "no". Ironically this became a little bit harder every time we overstepped a boundary.

For our next holiday, we'll ask Barbara for help. Beforehand, but also as a helpline during the trip. Barbara: "If someone calls on me at a time like that, my first task is to create peace. No one can think straight in a moment of panic. When a situation feels like a puzzle and all kinds of emotions start getting involved, it's very difficult to find a solution. As a coach, I'm a bit more detached from the situation and I'm not emotionally involved. That helps."

The wrong way

Unfortunately, not all my coaches were like Barbara. The worst coach I ever had was a lady who treated me like a little kid. We were going over my planning when the following conversation took place:

Coach: "What do you do in the morning?"
Me: "Ehm, I get up?"
Coach: "Yes, at what time?"
Me, self-employed and hardly ever using an alarm clock: "Ehm, I don't know?"
Coach: "And what do you do when you get up?"
Me: "Get dressed?"
Coach: "..."
Me: "..."
Coach: "You also need to shower and brush your teeth!"

Well, duh. Those things were so obvious to me I didn't even mention them, let alone put them in my daily planner. I'd lose my mind; I'd feel like the robot Naoki Higashida describes in his book. I'm sure there are people who won't take a shower unless you plan it for them, but I'm not one of those people, and my coach could have taken the trouble to check this beforehand.

I also had discussions with her about things like the Theory of Mind ("you don't have that") and a very uncomfortable conversation about relationships and living together, during which I had to assure her Riemer and I *absolutely* knew each other well enough and trusted each other. "Have you ever met his family, for example?" Riemer's parents spend most of the year in Thailand, so no, I'd never met them. "Have you ever had a huge fight?" No, we hadn't. Bad. Very bad.

Although it was useful to go over my weekly planning with her, I regularly had the feeling she underestimated me. She'd say things like: "Oh, you're a photographer, how unpredictable! Isn't that completely unsuitable for a person with autism?" I understand where she was coming from, but I think statements like that can be disastrous to autistics. Those who aren't overly confident, in particular, might think: "Hmm, never mind, I won't even try."

I've heard the same thing from several people, especially those who were diagnosed at a young age. On the one hand they're happy they got diagnosed early on: "Otherwise it really would have been one big mess", says Engelina, a girl in her twenties who was diagnosed at the age of five. "I was so different from the rest of the family, I thought I was adopted", comments Liza (25), who was diagnosed with autism in her first year of primary school.

On the other hand, there are the countless times they weren't taken seriously, not even by expert teachers and care workers. Engelina: "They wanted to send me to a special needs school, despite the fact I had no trouble learning. According to mental health care workers I would never graduate or live on my own. I have been living independently for a while now, with only two hours of help per week."

My ex Arnout got into a downward spiral and had to drop down several levels at high school because mental health care workers didn't care what he did, as long as he had some sort of daily activity. Liza was rejected for three different study programmes because of her autism. "And my family thought I wouldn't be able to plan our holiday because I'm autistic, even though I have no trouble planning things at all!"

It seems that people use a one-size-fits-all definition of autism without looking at the person in front of them. This is exactly why we need more visibility, more role models who don't fit the Rain Man image.

TIPS FOR PARENTS AND OTHER WANNABE COACHES

I think all parents are nervous when it comes to their child, autism or no autism. And I can imagine an autism diagnosis makes people even *more* protective. Maybe your heart was in your throat when you read about my Disney trip as a fifteen-year-old, my impulsive visit to Maan in Japan, or the failed trip with Riemer.

But in fact it's splurges like these that make me happiest of all. The trip to Disneyland when I was fifteen taught me to believe in my dreams. My trip to Tokyo taught me that taking risks can actually lead to something good. And even the failed holiday with Riemer taught me something: to speak up sooner. Something neither of us did during that trip, and we ended up paying the price. But there's nothing we can't overcome, and that in itself is a good lesson as well.

"My son is autistic. He recently went to a theme park on his own for the first time and now he wants to go to Tokyo. I'm terrified! Do you have any tips?"

A mother recently asked me this question. She wanted my expert opinion, as an autistic and a Tokyo fan. Her son, a verbal autistic eighteen-year-old of average intelligence, had been crazy about Japan for years. My advice: "Make sure he's well prepared and has a pocket wifi, and yell: "*Ganbatte!*" (Ganbatte is a Japanese cheer that means something like "Go for it!" or "Never give up!")

I understand that you're afraid as a parent. I also understand that a lot of people are prejudiced and think that we autistics aren't up to such things. That we function best in a 9-to-5 computer job and a daily planner scheduled to the brim. That's not always the case. It's also possible to have more of a global overview of things. If I know I can look things up, or how the timetable works, I don't need a specified itinerary. I find a plan that goes off the rails far more stressful than no plan at all.

Many autistic people know perfectly well what they want. And someone who knows what they want can achieve a lot. Work in a foreign country for example, like Arnout did. All people are in search of happiness, that's what gets you through life. Just staying holed up the whole time because you're afraid something might not work out? That'd make you *really* miserable. So your kid is crazy about roller coasters? Great! Encourage them! Count yourself lucky that your child has found something that brings them joy, and don't worry if they "can't make a decent living doing that". There's work in every industry and otherwise, your kid might make friends for life. I know people who run websites and podcasts about amusement parks. I know people who work there. I know people who visit meetups, organised by fan forums. And what about the engineers working at companies like Vekoma, designing rides?

"But what if my child can't handle it and has a breakdown?"

Ehm, well, shit happens. I still have mini-breakdowns on a regular basis. I even walked through Tokyo crying, when I got lost at Shinjuku station. You shouldn't try to prevent things like that.

What you *can* do is help them with a back-up plan, in case something *does* go wrong.

What always helps me, is to imagine the worst-case scenario. That may sound counterproductive, but most of the time the worst-case scenario isn't actually that bad – we usually get way more stressed when we stop thinking altogether.

I once missed a high-speed train in Paris, for example. Entirely my own fault, we left late and the metro took forever. You could get completely stressed out over a thing like this, of course, but what's the worst that can happen? Well, you'd have to buy a new ticket for the next one. And if it was the last train of the day, you'd need to book a hotel as well. A waste of money, sure. But not insurmountable, as long as a few basic requirements have been met:

1. You have enough money on you
2. You have a phone with internet access
3. There are people you can ask for help or advice

In fact, that's exactly what my mother told all those people who criticised her for letting me go to Disneyland Paris "by myself" (with my best friend) as a fifteen-year-old. We even took a touring car that dropped us off directly in front of the Disney hotel, so we were close to tour guides or Disney staff at all times. I had my brick of a cell phone and the money I had saved picking tomatoes. "Plus, if you stay home you still run the risk of a plane or a meteorite landing on your roof!" My mother's motto that always put everything into perspective reasoned me – an anxious child – out of bed on more than one occasion.

For autistic people who sometimes have trouble speaking, there's an app called Emergency Chat, which shows the reader a message explaining that the person in front of them is experiencing a meltdown. In the Netherlands we also have this in the form of a plastic card: the Autipas. With tools like these, a solution is always within reach. On top of that, most autistics I know aren't the type of people who don't look before they leap. Riemer, for example, always checks on Google Maps what the place he's about to visit looks like. I personally prefer to find out where the bathrooms are located. We know what we need in order to feel secure. You can trust us on that.

That goes for other things as well, by the way, like education. Don't ask: "Will you be able to handle that?" but "How are you going to tackle it when things get tough?" You don't have to finish a four-year course in four years. You can take longer if you need to. Look at what *is* possible, not at what isn't.

Chapter 6

Nothing about us, without us

You're reading a book about autism, written by someone who *has* autism. That may sound completely logical, but it wasn't like that for a long time. There's still a lot of talking about us, and very little listening to us. It's usually parents who appear in the media, it's usually scientists who aren't autistic themselves who study us as if we were some sort of exotic species.

With this book, I want to contribute to a change that is happening. An emancipation of autistics, who have a voice too – even those who can't speak. In the following chapters, I'll explain what organisations such as Autism Speaks are getting wrong, and I'll introduce you to the #ActuallyAutistic movement, which is trying to change the perception of autism.

Autism mums

The day after Halloween, a video went viral. An American mother filmed her eleven-year-old autistic, non-verbal son in a pizza costume, trick-or-treating. The little guy stands there, petrified, as one of his parents takes his finger and holds it up to a doorbell. "Usually, Halloween is a struggle, and I end up having to carry him home as my husband goes on with our other three kids. This year we finally got to celebrate Halloween as a family!", the mother wrote.

I was stunned to see the jubilant reactions it got. Sander (from chapter four) sent me the video: "Can you believe this?"

"Oh, the poor child", was my immediate reaction. Sander's thoughts exactly. We could both imagine just how terrifying it must have been for the little guy: ringing strangers' doorbells, and them answering the door in a weird costume, or loudly screaming "OH MY GOD ARE YOU A PIZZA?!!?!" The kid isn't even able to reply, which must make it even *more* painful. I understand why he had a meltdown the previous years.

I actually think it's worse that he *didn't* have a meltdown this year. Apparently the fear of disappointing his mother was even greater than his fear of trick-or-treating. Because there's no doubt that he understood: mummy wants to celebrate Halloween together. For once, mummy wants a normal family.

On my blog, I wrote about 'autism mums' before: mothers who are flaunting their children's autism, looking for sympathy and understanding, to such an extent that it seems autism has become *their* identity. A typical example is an interview with a famous Dutch actress in Dutch newspaper *De Volkskrant*, in which she says the following about her then two-year-old, intellectually disabled autistic son:

"*At some point, we're in his speech therapist's waiting room. He's playing with the door. I see he's about to get his finger caught in the door. Very slowly. Am I overcome by cruelty? Yes, it's cruel: I can do something, but I don't. I want to see how he responds to the pain. Is he going to scream? Will he come to me for comfort? Just like a normal child would? Because I don't know anymore.*

The door closes. Slowly. He doesn't cry, he doesn't scream. He seems surprised by the pain. He cries a lot, but never because he's sad. And not because of this awful pain either. Nothing is as it should be with him. I pull him out of the door, his little finger all bruised. I despise myself. Jesus, that's horrible. Do I even love my child?"[14]

It's bizarre. Not just the fact that she did this, but also that she describes it this way. Nobody would admit to dangling their kid off the balcony in a newspaper, out of fear of having Child Services called on them – yet she feels safe enough to

---

14 Duurvoort, Harriet. 'Mijn kind, mijn gevaarlijke kind' (interview with Romana Vrede), *De Volkskrant*, 2 July 2016

let this go to print. Even though she paints a picture of herself as a guilt-ridden parent who is aware of how awful her behaviour is, she trusts that most people will take pity on her. "It must be so hard, having an autistic child. Not surprising, then, that it makes you do crazy things sometimes."

She's not the only one: in an awareness campaign by Autism Speaks, the American organisation which claims to speak for autistics but mostly speaks for the bystanders, an 'autism mum' recounts how she wanted to drive off a bridge with her autistic child. She didn't do it in the end, because she had another, non-autistic child to care for. While she's telling this, the autistic child is behind her, frollicing around the room.

Time after time, autistic children are dehumanised. All sympathy goes to the parents because it's oh-so hard on them. Now I'm not trying to deny that, but aren't we forgetting someone? Aren't we forgetting the autistic child who's being dragged from door to door, the autistic child who gets his fingers stuck in the door because mummy isn't protecting him, and the autistic child who hears mummy wanted to kill her?

The Dutch actress made a theater show about her son. She talks about him in countless interviews – embarrassing, personal details and all. Her son is intellectually disabled and non-verbal; he can't convey what he thinks about this, except through his tantrums.

Now you might think: the kid is intellectually disabled, he doesn't think anything about this at all. But I wouldn't be too sure about that. The capacities of autistics often aren't equally distributed, which means that someone who doesn't speak and seemingly doesn't communicate, might still know exactly what you're saying. And even if that's not the case, such statements are harmful: they paint a picture that autistics aren't people and that they don't have feelings, let alone autonomy.

Schrödinger's autistic

After my post about autism mums, I received both criticism and support. Half of the critics said something along the lines of: "How can you – a high-functioning, working autistic – compare yourself to someone with the mental capacity of a three-year-old?!" The other half believed I was too autistic to understand the predicament of these hopeless mothers: "You probably lack the Theory of Mind to empathise with her situation!"

I was Schrödinger's autistic: both too autistic to understand, and not autistic enough to understand. Although autistics usually indicate they're happy about other autistics being outspoken, according to the autism mums, the pivotal point is right between verbal and non-verbal. According to them, we can't speak for non-verbal autistics, whereas they can. How very convenient.

However, when non-verbal or nearly non-verbal autistics do speak out, it turns out they suffer a lot because of the things autism mums say. There's nothing harder than feeling you're too much, Naoki Higashida writes in his book:

*"The hardest ordeal for us is the idea that we are caus-
ing grief for other people. We can put up with our own
hardships okay, but the thought that our lives are the
source of other people's unhappiness, that's plain
unbearable."*[15]

Although autism exists in various degrees, the issue is essen-
tially the same. I can speak, but I understand all too well why
that would be too intense for someone else. I don't tear my
clothes off, I don't bang my head on the wall, but I absolutely
understand why someone would want to do that. The difference between me and the aforementioned actress' son, for
example, is only partially down to the severity of our autism
– a much bigger difference is the mental disability. Such a
mental disability also makes autism a lot more visible: I can
reason that banging my head against the wall isn't going to
solve anything and will only make matters worse, and adjust
my behaviour – an intellectually disabled person might not.

So does that mean it's easy for *me* to say, because I *can*
say it? Because I'm intelligent, have a job and live independently? Those things certainly help. But they're not necessarily a means by which to measure someone's quality of
life. Many "high-functioning" autistics are depressed or sui-
cidal, or suffer from physical health issues caused by the
stress they experience on a daily basis. When I'm not doing
well, I sometimes dream of living in a group home where

---

15 Higashida, Naoki. *'The reason I jump'* Translated by K.A. Yoshida and
David Mitchell, 2013

everything is taken care of for me. It would save me a boat-load of stress.

And whether I lack empathy for those mothers? I have to admit that, initially, my main concern was for the kids. Especially because no one else seemed to care, and because they were more like me than the mothers gushing about them in the newspapers or on social media. I now do have a better understanding of what drives these mothers. I still think you're an idiot if you think it's okay to talk about your thoughts of murdering your child while said child is right there with you, but the mothers who go on about their kids' tantrums and meltdowns – they tend to be crying out for help.

When you're seeking specialised care, you're *expected* to go on about things – or risk not being taken seriously. And because getting the proper care can be a real pain in these times of reorganisations and financial cutbacks, these mums have usually already told their story hundreds of times, to hundreds of civil servants and healthcare workers, at hundreds of different institutions. Maybe, somewhere along the way, they simply forgot newspapers or the world-wide web aren't the right place to share these things.

#ActuallyAutistic

On social media, autistic people are using the hashtag #ActuallyAutistic to share their experiences. Please go check it out and make sure you follow a diverse set of people. This is the only way you'll get to learn about the variety of experiences people with autism go through.

One of the things the community is doing very well, is speaking out against Applied Behavioural Analysis (ABA), a form of therapy used mostly in the US (but sometimes in the Netherlands as well). This therapy, which, up to a few decades ago, was also commonly used to "cure" gay people, attempts to change behaviour by means of punishments and rewards.

Autistic children are sometimes "trained" up to forty hours a week: forty hours during which they're not allowed to flap their hands ("quiet hands!"), are forced to look the therapist in the eye and have to repeat words. Many autistics who underwent ABA describe the therapy as traumatic.

ABA therapy mainly focuses on compliance. Parents of autistic children are given pamphlets promising them they'll be able to take their child to a birthday party or to the shopping mall, just like "normal" families. According to the brochures, a life of horrors awaits those who don't choose ABA. There's a whole industry of highly paid coaches who get a full-time job out of each family.

Creating a horror scenario is the same business model Autism Speaks uses. Their 2009 video *I am autism* features music straight out of a horror movie, full of suspense and growing ever more intense, until a deep male voice addresses us ominously as if we're watching Anonymous claim a cyber hack: "I am autism... I'm visible in your children, but I'm not visible in you, until it's TOO LATE!" The voice threatens to take away your sleep, and your marriage. You'll never again be able to go to church or the park without being mortified, and you'll wither away in loneliness. In the second part of the video, the sun comes out, parents and family members in white T-shirts appear and the Big Bad Autism is strongly challenged: "You have underestimated us; we will beat you!" (Autism Speaks received a great deal of criticism for this campaign and has since drastically moderated their tone. But they continue to speak of autism as a "global health crisis" and are still pushing ABA as a desirable form of treatment, so they haven't won back my trust just yet.)

It's time to listen to autistics, instead of fearmongers. The fact that we're wired differently than the average person doesn't mean that our neurotype should be beaten or eradicated. What we want is more understanding for autistics – we would like people to respect our sensitivities and welcome our strengths.

In 2013 I decided to "come out" as autistic in a blogpost. It was scary as hell, because how was I to know if clients would still hire me? And would they use my autism against me by saying things like: "No no, you said you'd provide twelve more photos! You must have misunderstood because of your autism!"? I clicked 'Publish' and to my surprise, I got dozens of positive reactions, ranging from "What a brave thing to do!" to "I don't want anyone to know, but I have autism too." That last one in particular motivated me even more to speak up: nobody should feel forced to hide their autism.

TIP: How to find a therapy that fits

As you might have understood by now, many autistics disapprove of Applied Behavioural Analysis (ABA) therapy. They describe it as useless and downright abusive. A study by Henny Kupferstein found that children who underwent ABA therapy have a higher risk of PTSD than their peers.[16] Why is that, and what can a parent do to find a form of therapy that does work for their child?

First of all, think about your goal. Do you want this therapy for you, or for your child? Being able to take your child to a birthday party may sound like it's beneficial to them, but it's actually more about you. Are you looking for ways to prevent your child from experiencing sensory overload, or are you trying to teach

---

16 Kupferstein, H. (2018). Evidence of increased PTSD symptoms in autistics exposed to applied behavior analysis. *Advances in Autism*, 4(1), 19–29. DOI: 10.1108/AIA-08-2017-0016

your child how to endure it? Because the latter can be very, very harmful.

Ask yourself this: does this form of therapy take away any form of agency from my child? Imagine being trained for forty hours a week. If that's hard to imagine, take your first driving lesson, for example. You were probably exhausted after an hour – and you were (almost) an adult. When undergoing therapy, is your child able to say no? Is your child able to walk away? Will the therapist pick up on non-verbal cues that the child has had enough? I get that you might think it's helpful for your child to learn how to communicate their needs verbally, but do you teach your child how to swim by refusing to let them get out of the pool? I didn't think so.

An often-heard statement is that ABA therapy can make your child "indistinguishable from peers". But I'm begging you, don't aim for that. Your child is different, and they'll always be. And that's OK. By forcing them to be "normal", you're telling them you don't love them as they are. Autistic ways of playing are valid. So are autistic ways of communicating. Stimming is fine. Moving is fine.

By trying to change your child into someone else, you rob them of a very valuable sense: intuition. This will only make your child more vulnerable to exploitation. It's also becoming more and more clear that external rewards will diminish internal motivation, making your child actually less likely to learn or do something on their own.[17]

So please, kick the fearmongers out and look for professionals who accept your child and help them feel comfortable as they are.

---

17 Ulber J, Hamann K, Tomasello M. Extrinsic Rewards Diminish Costly Sharing in 3-Year-Olds. *Child Dev.* 2016;87(4):1192-1203. DOI: 10.1111/cdev.12534

Zjos' story:
The Perks Of Having A Dead Brother

Zjos Dekker (22) is autistic. She got diagnosed at the age of eighteen, even though care workers have known her all her life — as 'the sister of'. Her older brother and sister had autism, but Zjos didn't, or so the experts thought: she was "too social". A misconception that seems to trace back to the fact that from a very young age, Zjos was looking after her brother and sister, received training aimed at autistics' families, and accumulated a fairly sizeable collection of other diagnoses: a generalised anxiety disorder, dyslexia, dyscalculia and a disharmonic intelligence profile. She didn't make any friends in high school, but she came up with an explanation to her advantage: "I'm just way too smart for these people!"

Both on Twitter and on her blog *The Perks Of Having A Dead Brother*, she writes about her autism, her depression and her brother's death. Her harsh observations and her jokes about her dead brother make some people uncomfortable. He struggled so hard with his autism and depression that he eventually committed suicide.

"My goal in life is to make sure people don't have to commit suicide", Zjos writes on her blog. "Don't get me wrong, I'm pro-suicide", she says half-jokingly. "Because I don't want to betray my brother, and because I believe everyone is in charge of their own life." It's Zjos' way of coping with things.

"I want people to know what depression is, and that it's not your fault." The former theatre student wants to get rid of taboos by stepping into the spotlight and speaking openly about her depression and her autism on radio and television. By doing this, she hopes to encourage people to seek help in time, so they won't have to go down the same path as her brother.

With thousands of followers on Twitter and several radio and TV appearances under her belt, Zjos is well on her way. She's doing a lot better with regard to her depression as well, now that she has gotten the right mental health care and tools to help get her life back on track. She currently lives on her own with the help of an assisted-living programme and has a part-time job in psychiatric care which allows her to utilise both her experiences with autism and her knowledge of (social) media.

Every time someone tries to argue that people like Zjos and me have it easy because we're "high-functioning", I think of her brother. He would have been considered "high-functioning" too. But he's dead.

Christina's story: growing up in the spotlight

Christina Curry, the daughter of MTV host, internet entre-preneur and podcasting co-inventor Adam Curry and Dutch singer and showbiz diva Patricia Paay, grew up in the spot-light. When she was twelve years old, her family starred in the reality show *Adam's Family* and in the years following, she featured in all kinds of shows and gossip columns. "I came out of the womb overstimulated", Christina jokingly said to Filemon Wesselink in his TV show *Het is hier autistisch* (It's autistic here).

In 2015, Christina announced she's autistic by writing about it in a column. "I saw a psychiatrist and ended up scor-ing very high on the autism scale. I already had my suspicions because it's prevalent on my father's side of the family. To top it all off, I also turned out to have pretty severe OCDs."

Christina has always had the feeling she was different and often felt distant and nervous as a child. Yet nobody saw her as autistic.

"In my teens I was told there was nothing wrong with me. I looked normal, and that of course means you're totally fine. Except I wasn't: I would pick at the skin on my arms and my face for hours in an attempt to calm my worried mind. It was so bad even that I was covered in bruises and scabs, and I ended up not wanting to go outside unless I wore a thick lay-er of makeup to hide all the marks. On top of that, my obses-sive thoughts and my compulsions were driving me crazy.

It saddens me sometimes that the whole country got such

a close look into my private life during my teenage years. I said and did a lot of weird things. Sometimes to shock people, but more often because I couldn't foresee the consequences of my actions. I was angry and aggressive because I couldn't deal with other people's emotions and because things didn't go the way I wanted."

She doesn't blame anyone for the fact that her autism wasn't discovered until later in her life. Christina: "I guess I could be mad at my parents for not recognising the symptoms of autism and neurosis earlier on, but let's be honest, being a parent is just really hard. Especially when your child is quite eccentric by nature."

Thankfully, Christina is doing a lot better since she got diagnosed: "It was tricky at first, because I felt the diagnosis merely emphasised that there was something wrong with me. I've learnt a lot since then. I no longer force myself to go to events or places that are triggers for me or cause sensory overload, and when I do get overstimulated, I talk about it. But nowadays I'm just as happy to stay home with my girlfriend and our bunnies."

In *Het is hier autistisch*, Christina talks about how much she enjoys seeing people who are extremely interested in one specific topic. I, in turn, enjoy seeing Christina enthusiastically explain why she knows everything there is to know about the song *Jessie's Girl* and how that even led to her getting singer Rick Springfield's name tattooed on her arm. She now has a new obsession: astrology. "My friends are joking I'm going 'full auti' again, haha!"

Since she "came out" as autistic, Christina has had a lot of reactions: "I got a lot of really sweet messages from people who were happy to now have a role model like me because they saw themselves in me. Many people still associate autism with a guy in his thirties who lives in his parents' basement and spends the whole day behind his computer. I think it's important that we focus more on autism in women. Lots of people are familiar with autistic obsessions like trains and action figures, but young girls who are autistic will often show an extreme interest in, say, a certain boy band or actor.

Another misconception I'd like to clear up is that people with autism supposedly lack empathy. I for one am very intuitive, and 90% of the time I'm open to other people's emotions. The other 10% of the time I'm so lost in my own thoughts and obsessions, virtually nothing else gets through."

Apart from the nice messages, Christina also received some negative reactions. "They were from people who thought I had just labelled myself to get attention. Because – you guessed it – I didn't look autistic at all!"

Chapter 7

Eight things we don't want to hear anymore

There are certain comments autistics hear all the time. Misconceptions and generalisations we hear *so* often, the time has come to bust them once and for all. For starters, the title of this book, the sentence that makes every autistic person's skin crawl: "But you don't look autistic at all!"

1 But you don't look autistic at all!

"Autism is like this cream: invisible." The head of the Dutch Autism Society made this comparison to a jar of Kiehl's at a fundraiser for the Autism Foundation. People often say: "You can't see autism." I'll let you in on a little secret: I often *do* see autism.

Autism isn't like Down Syndrome, where you're born with specific physical features. At first glance, autistics seem "normal". But their posture, motions and eyes often give away that something's up. Autistic movements may include repetitive motions, clapping or flapping one's hands or other so-called stims. Due to our lack of sensory integrations, many autistics have bad posture. We just can't seem to construct one whole out of our many limbs. This might also be the reason why we bump into table corners more often than the average person, and regularly drop things.

Because many autistics experience a lot of stress, our posture may appear stiff: our muscles contract and don't release. This is why it sometimes looks like my shoulders are attached to my ears. Well, not literally. But they're up high and they hurt.

Autistic people can have a skittish look in their eyes, or avoid eye contact. As I wrote earlier, making eye contact is a lot more intense for autistics than it is for the average person. Those who do want to look at people often stare at the bridge of someone's nose or at someone's eyebrow. For too long sometimes, which might make the other person think they have ketchup on their face.

Although virtually all autistics are affected by the things I just mentioned, a lot of autistic people have taught themselves to suppress them due to societal pressure. You won't see me waving my hands like it's 1999, for instance. It's all too clear to us autistics that someone who's stimming by twirling around while waving their arms in order to make that weird body feel a little better, will be perceived as strange. Children receiving behavioural therapy according to the ABA method are often forced to sit still and look the therapist in the eye. "Quiet hands" (an ABA term that means your child isn't stimming) are rewarded. We get the message: what you're doing is wrong. If you don't want to be bullied or be seen as a freak, do as we do. Normal. As the Dutch saying goes: "Act normal, that's crazy enough."

And then, after years of bullying, being "weird" and fighting pretty much all of your natural impulses, resulting in headaches, stress and psychological problems, you've done it. A random stranger who you've just told you're autistic, comments: "But you don't look autistic at all!"

Ehm... thanks?

My head is spinning. I don't look autistic at all. Does she think I'm exaggerating? No, she said it in a nice way. It sounds like a compliment. She's smiling. Is that an accomplishment? Is it a good thing if you don't look autistic?

After years of adjusting, compensating, and hiding, I would much rather finally be able to be myself for once, if I still know how to. But when I am myself, I look more autistic. And apparently, that's not okay. Or something.

How autistic someone looks doesn't say much about how autistic someone is. All it does is give an indication of how intelligent someone is and how much that person has been "trained" to show neurotypical behaviour. For that reason, most non-autistic-looking autistics tend to be the people who experience the highest psychological pressure. Their brain is running non-stop on full capacity, their self-monitoring is so internalised the system can't actually be turned off anymore. A constant flow of information (at best) or heartless self-criticism (at worst) leaves the owner of this brain overworked, burnt-out and depressed.

"But you don't look autistic at all!" says Janet-who-doesn't-know-me-at-all. "She means well!" my brain corrects. She means well.

2 Are you sure you're not an Indigo child?

A while ago I received an email via the contact form on my blog: "Are you sure you have Asperger's? The first thing I noticed in your cute, cheeky eyes was that you're a hyper-sensitive person, probably an Indigo child…" By then my eyebrows were somewhere around my hairline. What the…? "Curious to hear what you think", the sender concluded.

I had to think about it for a full month. From my very first impulse, screenshotting the email and dumping the entire thing on social media and via a mild "but she means well, doesn't she?", I arrived at the question that took longest to answer: What exactly is it that I find so infuriating?

I think it has to do with the reason some people want to relabel autism, an official diagnosis, to the 'HSP' (Highly Sensitive Person) personality type, or worse, empty new-age terms such as 'Indigo child': they link autism to a ton of negative prejudices they'd rather not be associated with. "Autistics? You mean those annoying sociopaths who don't have any feelings? On the contrary, I feel an awful lot! When you stub your toe, I'm already crying! That's how much I feel!"

Thankfully it's not 1950 anymore, and we now know more about autism. One thing that's become clear is that we aren't insensitive robots, but we may seem that way sometimes because we close ourselves off. Stimuli – and that includes emotions – are often so intense for autistics that they have developed a defense mechanism.

Because autism is a spectrum disorder, highly sensitive people might well be a little closer to the autistic end than the average person – not quite as good at processing stimuli as the average person, but not bad enough to be full-blown autistic. Or maybe they are, but they just don't like the label.

And that's what bothers me the most: if everyone thinks the label 'autistic' is too negative and starts coming up with more interesting names, people will only see autism in a more and more negative light. Because all those beautiful, sensitive, vulnerable and creative people, no, they are *highly sensitive*! It's only angry teenagers and stupid ex-husbands who are autistic.

Get out of here. Hypersensitivity is part of my autism. It's a blessing and a curse; something that makes *me* different, but also something that makes me me. My "cute, cheeky eyes" are still cute and cheeky if what they tell you is that I have autism.

And an Indigo child? According to a random new-age website I checked, Indigo children are "clairsentient and telepathic", they have "a soul that has lived many lives", "their top two chakras are open wide" and they are "more emotional than rational". I'm sorry, but my rational autistic brain thinks this is bullshit.

"Now, now, Toeps, do you have to be so vulgar? That sweet lady meant well, didn't she?" Maybe she did. But to diagnose someone based on their "cute, cheeky eyes" and three blog posts is dangerous. If someone doesn't get the correct diagnosis or believes sensory overload can be fixed by an aura spray or charged crystals, they run the risk of a burn-out or other health issues. The email also reveals the subconscious prejudices of the author – prejudices my "cute, cheeky eyes" and I are more than happy to debunk.

3 Didn't your mother love you enough?

It's astonishing to think that there's a Dutch autism institute that still carries the name of Leo Kanner, a psychiatrist who became a renowned autism expert between the 1930s and the 1960s. In 1943, Kanner claimed that autism was caused by a lack of parental love. "Such mothers defrost just long enough to bring a child into this world", he told Time Magazine. Kanner's contemporary Bruno Bettelheim also supported this concept.

Kanner's and Bettelheim's ideas resounded in the medical world for a long time. And even when, in the 70s, it turned out there was no such thing as a "refrigerator mother", lots of parents still viewed parents of autistic children with suspicion. "Give me that kid for a week, I'll teach him how to behave!" is something a lot of parents of autistic children still hear regularly.

The classic image of the refrigerator mother has slowly shifted to a different accusation: mothers who are over-ambitious, and don't have time for a 'difficult' child. And when it's not the mother, it's the teacher who's to blame. "It's easier to diagnose the child than it is to ask yourself what you, as a school or a family, can do to give children who are different more room", Sanne Bloemink writes in an op-ed, in which she argues that too many kids get a diagnosis these days. "And why hasn't anyone noticed that the girl who gets tested endlessly for autism is severely neglected by her parents?"[18]

It's supposed to all be down to our out-of-control performance-driven society, in which all children have to be excellent. Although Bloemink addresses an important issue here, I think it's extremely dangerous to throw the baby out with the bathwater.

Getting the right diagnosis is a very important step in improving the quality of life of autistics. You don't gain anything by getting a diagnosis, but it does help with your self-acceptance and with finding solutions that work for you. Of course not every autistic is the same, but there are similarities. If you know where to look, you don't have to start from scratch every time. That will save you a lot of stress.

---

18 Bloemink, Sanne. 'Laat die diagnose eens zitten en kijk hoe een kind wel tot bloei komt', *De Volkskrant*, 26 October 2018

4 I always colour coordinate the shirts in my closet; I'm *so* autistic!

No honey, you're not. You're just neat. Yay you.

It happens all the time: people using 'autistic' as a character trait, as a description, or as a synonym for 'rigid' or 'difficult'. Dutch Minister of Economic Affairs Eric Wiebes, for example, said in reference to the gas extraction debacle in the north of the Netherlands: "We don't have to be autistic about it." He later apologised for it, but this statement is a perfect example of how many people think.

Autism is not the same as plain rigidity. Someone who isn't flexible isn't necessarily autistic. And if you jokingly describe yourself as 'autistic', you're short-changing people who *do* have autism. Because autism is much more than that, as you can tell from the DSM-5 diagnostic criteria at the beginning of this book.

Someone who organises their closet 'autistically' probably doesn't have a meltdown when there's a shirt out of place. Neurotypical people tend to be able to overlook things like that. Watering down the term autism like this creates a lot of ambiguity for the general public. You can't turn off real autism. You don't choose it, and whoever tries to get over it, pays the price for it later.

5 Everybody wants a label nowadays

Could it be that he's autistic? This is the question Dutch presenter Filemon Wesselink set out to answer in his show "Het is hier autistisch" ("It's autistic here"). In the first episode, he answers a long list of questions by a professor at Radboud University. Yes, Wesselink agreed, whenever he watches TV, he always changes the channels in the same order. As a young boy, he preferred to play with Lego by himself and nowadays when he finds himself in a busy bar, he often goes to the bathroom just to be by himself for a moment. Well, the Radboud University professor concludes, this could be indicative of autism. Practically giddy, Wesselink sits up straight: "Really?!"[19]

This piece is the intro for an article in Dutch newspaper *de Volkskrant*, written by Margot C. Pol. Apart from the fact that this is quite simplistic (he wasn't diagnosed after this one short conversation, but after extensive research and conversations with Filemon's mother and partner), Pol also fills in all kinds of things herself. She sees Filemon's surprise as happiness: he's "practically giddy", according to her. Pol wonders: is it me, or does everyone have a mental disorder nowadays?

---

19 Margot C. Pol. 'Wie is er nog normaal?', *Volkskrant Magazine*, 8 April 2017

> *It gets easier and easier to officially 'have' something:
> [...] Take the autism spectrum disorder (ASD), the offi-
> cial term for autism, for instance. To diagnose ASD,
> someone needs to have impaired social communica-
> tion skills and show repetitive behaviour – who doesn't
> have or exhibit things like that?*

I'm astounded this article made it past final editing, because
this is an outright lie – remember the DSM criteria on page
18? Pol completely ignores the fact that one of the requirements for an ASD diagnosis is that the symptoms severely
affect your daily life, and that they can't be explained in any
other way. If you're at a party where you feel uncomfortable
because you don't know anyone, there's no way that'll get
you diagnosed with autism, like Pol pretends.

Next up is Belgian psychoanalyst Paul Verhaeghe, who
sees diagnoses as a welcome excuse: "Does your wife want
a divorce after twenty years? Not your fault, you just can't
empathise with her very well because of your autism." I wonder how Verhaeghe thinks this "excuse" helps a guy like that:
he's still divorced. It can be useful to know the reason why,
but that's about all a diagnosis will give you. Well, perhaps
a slight reduction in self-hatred, because you used to think
you were just a total loser who needed to quit whining. "Just
stop whining", is also psychiatrist Bram Bakker's solution in
this article.

Is ASD diagnosed more often than it used to be?
Absolutely. But that's mainly because we know more now,
which helps us recognise autism sooner. The fact that fewer

people were diagnosed back in the day doesn't mean that the ones who *weren't* diagnosed were doing just fine. I'm thinking of Elfriede and Margarete, the two girls being treated by Hans Asperger, who were viewed as "hormonal and suffering from severe behavioural deficiencies" and sent to the Am Spiegelgrund clinic.

Do we really have to start battling this ignorance again? Battling the people who, thanks to Pol's article, will cross every boundary with cliches such as "everybody has something" and "just stop whining"? And is it better that undiagnosed autistics never find out what's the matter with them, so that they keep running into the same problems over and over again until they've lost all self-esteem? The goal of the "label" isn't to make us feel oh-so special. The label is a diagnosis that finally puts a name to what we always knew was there. So that we can move on.

6 I don't believe in labels, you're just you!

A few weeks ago, I read a tweet. A sixteen-year-old girl had told her physiotherapist she was autistic, to which the therapist had replied: "I don't like labels." An undoubtedly well-intentioned lady responded to this tweet with: "Maybe your therapist meant: 'I just see you as a human being'?"

Those who aren't familiar with autism, may not immediately see the problem here. "Surely that's a good thing? Seeing everyone as an individual?" Absolutely. But what I'm trying to show with this example is that statements like these are proof of subconscious prejudices; prejudices that actually rob the autistic girl of her individuality.

The physiotherapist doesn't like labels. Do you think she goes to work every day in a metal transportation vehicle on four wheels that runs on fossil fuel? No, of course not, because labels serve a purpose. There's a massive difference between a Ferrari and a Fiat Panda, but the label 'car' at least gives an indication. The label 'autism' works the same way.

The girl let her therapist know that she's autistic, to explain why she might respond differently to touch or to instructions. She was probably hoping her physio would know something about autism and would adjust her behaviour accordingly, for example by warning the girl before touching her. By immediately shutting down this conversation opener, the physiotherapist sends a signal that she's not willing to learn more about her patient.

Now you might think, "Couldn't the girl have just asked for a warning before the therapist touched her? There's no need to drag the diagnosis into this, is there?" True, she could have done that. But do you really want to dictate how a sixteen-year-old raises her issues? There's a good chance she tried that method before and that someone told her not to be a baby about it, or that it wouldn't be so bad. She probably mentioned her autism to convince the physiotherapist of the seriousness of the situation. Sometimes you just can't get it right, no matter what you do.

And what about the response on Twitter? "Maybe your therapist meant: 'I just see you as a human being'?" It probably wasn't meant this way but I can't help wondering: aren't autistics human beings too? The two aren't mutually exclusive, are they? Someone who tells you they are autistic is still just a human being with a personality, experiences and feelings. If you have to reject someone's autism in order to see them as a human being, you're ignoring an intrinsic part of that person to avoid having to deal with something that makes you uncomfortable.

7 You're not autistic, you have au-tis-m

"As the parent of an autistic child I believe that atypical is the new normal — and that seeing things differently can help us all move forward", American democratic presidential candidate Andrew Yang wrote on Twitter. Almost immediately the backlash started: "Mr. Yang, don't you know it's 'with autism'? This way of speaking will cost you votes!"

You've probably noticed that throughout this book, I have used the terms 'autistic' and 'autistic person', but sometimes also 'person with autism'. The choice of words is a hot topic nowadays, leading to endless feuds.

Most autistics prefer to be called just that: autistic. A lot of parents and professionals on the other hand, are taught that it's better to say 'person with autism' — so-called person-first-language. They think that by addressing us this way, they're saying we're a person too, not just our autism. Many autistic people disagree, because they feel that 'autistic' *is* who they are: their autism is an essential part of their being. That's identity-first-language. To them, 'person with autism' sounds like 'person with a disease'. Something that needs a cure. They don't need a cure, they need understanding. And I totally agree with that.

Yet I have used 'person with autism' on several occasions throughout this book. There are multiple reasons for this. First, there are people who *do* like to be called 'person with autism' because they feel like 'autistic' is kind of a slur. (I guess this is more so in Dutch; 'een autist' in Dutch sounds way harsher than 'an autistic' in English – but even in English, around 10% of the community prefers 'with autism'.)

Second, I really believe that intent matters. I also believe that I, as an autistic person myself, can describe myself however I want. And I don't believe in the excessive policing of other people's speech. It distracts from the message.

Sometimes 'people with autism' just works better in a sentence. That doesn't imply I believe that 'people with autism' need to be cured. On the other hand, I also don't believe 'autistic people' means we are only that and have no other distinctive traits. It should be obvious that we're complex people, and that there will always be other factors at play.

Personally I don't care that much about what you call me. But what I can't stand is neurotypical people who feel the need to decide *for* me how I should be addressed. Like the people responding to Andrew Yang, or the GP who got mad at the Dutch newspaper NRC because they used the headline 'An autistic on jihad' above an article about a twenty-four-year-old autistic guy from Zoetermeer who travelled to Syria. The NRC apologised, despite the fact that the boy's parents said they had no problem with the headline.

The NRC's ombudsman made a side note in his analysis, with which I agree wholeheartedly: "Describing a person with a noun is not a complete identification, let alone an exclusive one. A communist *isn't* communism, a teacher is not the same as their teachings. There are dozens of ways to describe people, none of which are exhaustive." Or, as I like to say: a painter is not just a painter. An autistic is a human being. That should be so evident, we shouldn't need to play word games over this.

8 It's probably because of the vaccinations

No.

Epilogue: Pick your battles

More and more autistics are speaking out, #ActuallyAutistic is a thing, and institutions are slowly starting to understand they need to listen to people with autism. There's another trend happening, however, that has me very worried. Although I'm glad we are raising awareness in people, I also see self-advocates nowadays who are *so* angry, there's no way of getting it right. I'll give you an example.

Some time ago a supermarket introduced 'stimuli-free mornings'. On those mornings, the music is turned off, all the shelves are neatly arranged, the cash registers don't beep and there are no shelf stackers wheeling large trolleys down the aisles. This would make it a bit easier for autistic people, among others, to do their grocery shopping. Great, you'd think. Someone on Twitter responded: "Pfff. I find this incredibly stigmatising. Now I have to go to the supermarket on this particular morning? I just want them to always be considerate of me!"

To an extent, I can understand that this would rub some people the wrong way. We autistics encounter ignorance on a daily basis, and that's frustrating. I've thought about this long and hard, because on the one hand I want to advise people not to take things so seriously and to learn to just shrug it off. But on the other hand it feels like this is going against my ideals. Is it possible to want things to improve, but to shrug things off at the same time? The answer is yes.

The difference is whether you look at this from a society perspective or an individual perspective. I'm an idealist when it comes to society, I'm a pragmatist on a personal level. This helps me to stay happy, because if you focus non-stop on everything that is wrong with society – and that's a lot! – you will only end up incredibly frustrated. Does this mean I'm burying my head in the sand? I don't think so. I'm writing this book. I have a blog. I recently did a series of photos for the Dutch Autism Society's (NVA) forty-year anniversary.

During the days of the photo shoot, even the NVA seemed to forget they were working with autistics at times. "Could you just quickly take a photo of me too?" one staff member asked me, completely ignoring my well-crafted schedule. "I need it for an interview!" My first impulse was to get angry. There are autistics who wouldn't have taken the job in the first place, because the NVA undoubtedly published some alleged "problematic" tweets or news items in the past. But I'm a pragmatist: what would be most helpful? Explaining my situation and point of view, I decided. I chose to take the picture, but I did explain afterwards that I wasn't entirely happy with how things went. The organisation said they understood and promised to be more considerate in the future.

There are people who think it isn't my job to educate people. That's true – it's my choice to do this. And to be clear – I don't believe we *have* to do this. But just being angry at the world all the time doesn't get you anywhere either, as I learnt years ago.

At the time of my eating disorder, I was in group therapy with some girls who, to put it mildly, weren't crazy about the fashion industry. All those skinny models, that had to change.

They blamed fashion magazines for their eating disorders and were convinced their lives would be a lot better if those magazines featured models in all shapes and sizes on their covers. Although, socially speaking, this would be a good thing of course (something I also strive for in my own work as a photographer), at the individual level, the girls had to learn to adopt a different attitude. They had to learn to shrug it off, to stop buying those magazines, and to not let those ads get to them. One of our therapists said: "If you're waiting for the fashion magazines to change, you're giving away all control over your eating disorder." That's the same attitude you can choose to have when it comes to autism.

Autistic people are different. They just happen to be a minority who live in a world that's geared towards people with a stronger filter for stimuli. And although I believe we should all be considerate towards each other as much as possible, the interests of autistics and neurotypicals are sometimes diametrically opposed. Most people *like* music in the supermarket; they think it creates a nice atmosphere. You can't design a supermarket where music is and isn't played at the same time, so you'll have to designate special mornings for autistics. Or wear noise-cancelling headphones. Or start ordering your groceries online. I have accepted that I'm different, and I have found solutions that work for me. I try to create more understanding for autism so the cashier doesn't think I'm rude when I stand in front of her with my headphones on and don't say anything back. But is that what she's really thinking? Then I shrug. Her problem, not mine.

So, my dear fellow autistics reading my book: please, pick your battles. Do it for your own peace of mind, for your own happiness. Keep in mind that a lot of people just know very little about autism, but that doesn't mean there's something wrong with who you are. Give them this book to read if they're interested, and if they're not, that's fine too. It's great when people understand you, but it is not always essential. Live your life, make your choices, and do it for yourself. You're okay.

Printed in Great Britain
by Amazon

82072531R00130